Issues in Focus

Body Image
A Reality Check

Pamela Shires Sneddon

Enslow Publishers, Inc.

40 Industrial Road   PO Box 38
Box 398   Aldershot
Berkeley Heights, NJ 07922   Hants GU12 6BP
USA   UK

http://www.enslow.com

Library of Congress Cataloging-in-Publication Data

Sneddon, Pamela Shires.
    Body image : a reality check / Pamela Shires Sneddon.
        p. cm. — (Issues in focus)
    Includes bibliographical references and index.
    Summary: Discusses the problems with body image, the reasons why some people have a poor body image, and how self-perception and self-acceptance are affected by society.
    ISBN 0-89490-960-6
    1. Body image in adolescence—Juvenile literature. 2. Self-acceptance in adolescence—Juvenile literature. [1. Body image. 2. Self-acceptance. 3. Self-perception.] I. Title. II. Series: Issues in focus (Springfield, N.J.)
    BF724.3.B55S54   1999
    155.9'2—dc21   98-35120
                                                    CIP
                                                    AC

J 155.92

Printed in the United States of America

10 9 8 7 6 5 4 3 2

To Our Readers:
All Internet addresses in this book were active and appropriate when we went to press. Any comments or suggestions can be sent by e-mail to Comments@enslow.com or to the address on the back cover.

Illustration Credits: © Convenant Education Offices, 1997, used by permission, p. 9; © Corel Corporation, pp. 19, 28, 34, 64, 93, 96; Derick Larkin, p. 17; © Díamar Interactive Group, pp. 31, 42; Doug Heller, p. 36; Enslow Publishers, Inc., 73; Jennifer Thompson, pp. 10, 39, 45, 48, 91; Kristen and Chris Sneddon, pp. 77, 80 ; Library of Congress, p. 30; Matthew Sneddon, p. 89; Pamela Sneddon, pp. 56, 59; Robert M. Friedman, p. 7; Scott Miller, p. 23.

Cover Illustration: Jennifer Thompson.

Contents

Acknowledgments

Special thanks to the professionals who shared from their experience for this book: Dr. Steven J. Anderson, chairperson, American Academy of Pediatrics Committee on Sports Medicine and Fitness; Dr. Myrna L. Armstrong, professor, School of Nursing, Texas Tech University; Tim Connelly, women's cross-country coach, University of Notre Dame; Carolyn Costin, director, Eating Disorder Center of California; Dr. Dean Given; Jon Ireland, youth minister, Montecito Covenant Church; Dr. Michael Levine, professor of psychology, Kenyon College; Dr. Louise Ousley, Student Health Center, University of California at Santa Barbara; Dr. John Persing, professor and chief of plastic surgery, Yale University Medical School; Dr. Steven Popkow; Dr. Don Roberts, professor of communications, Stanford University; Dr. Barbara Staggers, medical director, adolescent medicine, Children's Hospital, Oakland, California; Jeri Waite, nutritionist, eating disorder consultant; Dr. Ed Wimberly; and Monika Wooley, president, Better Way Health Control, Phoenix, Arizona.

Thanks also to the students in Gloria Sanchez's health classes at Santa Barbara Junior High School and the other teens across the country who helped with questionnaires. I'm grateful as well to Jane Steltenpohl, Stephanie Cannon, Jennifer Thompson, and to my family for their help with content and photographs.

Although comments in the book are from real teenagers, many names have been changed to protect their privacy.

1

Body Image—
What, Exactly,
Is It?

Fifteen-year-old Josie describes herself like this: "My thighs make me look like an elephant. And that's what I feel like—a great big elephant."

Thirteen-year-old Mac says, "I would stay home from school if I had to shower after gym in front of all the other guys."

Sixteen-year-old Erica confides, "My mom and dad finally agreed to let me have a nose job. I've always wanted one, ever since the kids started calling me Hawkface."

On the other hand, eight-year-old Eddie had no doubt in his confident voice when he asked, "Mirror, mirror on the wall. Who's the coolest dude of all?" As he held up his completed art project, thirty little mirrors glued onto a wooden frame twinkled back thirty little Eddies, and they all looked perfect. At the age of eight, Eddie has a great body image.

Body image, or the way we perceive our physical selves, can change drastically between childhood and the teenage years. Puberty brings with it radical shifts in body shape, weight, hormonal balance, and sex characteristics. All these physical changes, combined with the ordinary stresses of growing up and becoming independent, can set off a major upheaval in the life of any teen.

If you are a teenager, your body image can overshadow everything else in your life. As a child, you took your body image for granted. How you appeared to others, or to yourself, was not as important as what your body could do. From an early age, you were encouraged by your family, teachers, and friends when you mastered a physical challenge. Learning to crawl, walk, swim, use a crayon, ride a bike, and throw a ball were almost always rewarded with at least as much praise as looking cute or wearing a pretty outfit. How and when did all that change?

An Outgrowth of Emotions

As the brain organizes information it receives from the senses—sight, hearing, touch, smell—it sifts the information through the screen of experience each person has developed over the various stages of life. Everyone's experience starts with how we are held and touched as infants, and how we are taught to

Learning to walk is one of a toddler's earliest challenges. By mastering physical tasks and controlling the space around them, children achieve a positive body image.

control our bodies as children. At first, babies make no distinction between their own bodies and their mothers' bodies. Then, as toddlers, their bodies become separate and distinct and are used to explore the physical world. Positive body image or self-perception is attained by mastering simple tasks and controlling the space around us.

In addition, our body image is formed by how others judge our physical appearance. Parents and caretakers have an immense impact on how we see and judge our physical selves. Parents can reinforce whether or not we stress one particular body part as superior or inferior. Likewise, they have the power to make us feel, from the earliest age, that our bodies are shameful and dirty, or beautiful and natural.

How you see your physical body mentally, and how satisfied you are with that mental picture, are both just as important to your body image, perhaps more so, than how your body actually is. Body image concerns not only your actual form—weight, height, and shape—but what you see inside your head when you look in the mirror. It also concerns the way you think others see you.

Our emotions play a large part in determining our body image. People who are generally more content tend to be less self-judging. The reverse is also true. According to one study, children who were made to experience failure as all-important pictured them-selves as being shorter than they actually were.[1]

"Everyone has a body image and it has strong emotional overtones based on our experiences in life," wrote David Garner and Ann Kearney-Cooke in

Body image is a prime concern during the teenage years—but it's only part of a person's identity.

Psychology Today magazine. "Our image of our body plays a major role in how we feel, what we do, whom we meet, whom we marry, and what career path we choose, even if its precise meaning and its role in mental well-being continue to elude psychologists."[2]

Forming an Identity

To a teenager, body image is especially important. At a time when everything in one's life is changing dramatically and rapidly, the approval of others becomes paramount. Sometimes body image becomes the only measure teens use to compare themselves to others.

All other character qualities—social skills, intellectual gifts, spirituality—may take a back seat. This is a time kids are going through a transition between being dependent on parents and standing on their own, says Deborah Webb Blackburn, a psychologist in Virginia. "To make the transition, kids have to feel like they are part of a group. The way to belong at this age is to look like everyone else."[3]

The biggest task faced by adolescents during this

New adult physical traits make teens feel self-conscious and encourage them to compare themselves to others to see how they measure up.

time of transition is the formation of a personal identity. Psychiatrist Erik Erikson said that during this crucial stage a person needs to develop an increasing sense of "being at home in one's body, a sense of 'knowing where one is going,' and an inner assuredness of anticipated recognition from those who count." Erikson added that such a sense of identity is difficult to achieve, that it takes time, and that if it doesn't happen during this adolescent stage of life, the issues of adulthood are more difficult to cope with.[4]

The dramatic physical changes that happen during adolescence—breast development, the beginning of menstruation, growth spurts, voice changes, and the growth of facial and pubic hair— generally make a teen feel anything but "at home in one's body." Being unaccustomed to new, adult physical traits only encourages teens to compare themselves to others. They want to see how they measure up, both to their peers and to adults. Often they feel they've fallen short in both fields. And, as if this intense self-inspection were not enough, teasing and exclusion by peers make teens doubt their worth even more. Girls who mature earlier than others are commonly at risk of feeling out of sync with their friends and are more likely to be teased and even sexually harassed by the boys. Similarly, boys who mature later than their peers often feel inferior to the other, more adult-looking males.

Youth minister Jon Ireland, who works with adolescents in Montecito, California, sees how stressful this period is for teens. "They worry when they aren't on the same biological track as their peers," he says. He is quick to point out, however, that this is not a new problem. "I remember as a high school student, every day looking at my armpits. I was in the tenth grade—how come I didn't have any hair under my arms? I was one of those late bloomers, but it really worried me."[5]

In our modern culture teenage girls face unique pressures. Studies have shown that many girls experience a dramatic drop in self-esteem as they become teenagers. Emily Hancock, a psychologist in Berkeley, California, said that her studies, based on interviews with dozens of high school and college girls, revealed that self-esteem in girls peaks at the age of nine, then begins to fall off quickly. She found that girls gradually lose their preteen confidence and become increasingly critical of the way they look.[6]

Psychologists feel that when girls try to weigh the messages they are getting from the media, society, and their peers about how they should be against their own inner doubts, many can't help but feel inferior.[7] This holds especially true for the pressures to conform to an ideal body type.

Although studies show that males do not undergo exactly the same stresses as females to conform to a perfect body image, there are still indications that boys, too, are worrying more about their body image than they did in previous generations. One observer wrote, ". . . [There] seems to be emerging a single standard of beauty for men today: a hypermasculine, muscled, powerfully shaped body—the Soloflex man. It's an open question whether that standard will become as punishing for men as has women's superthin standard."[8] Out of seventeen junior high school students interviewed, ten said being tall was a crucial trait of being an attractive man. Having a muscular, strong body or a washboard stomach was also important.[9]

"People with a negative body image worry constantly about how they look," says Richard Gordon, professor of psychology at Bard College. "It affects their confidence and self-esteem."[10]

With the increased pressure from the modern media on teenagers to conform to an ideal body type, there is a growing risk of endangering their health. As a result of comparing themselves to the male and female ideals shown constantly on television and in magazines and the movies, most teens can't help but find fault with their appearance. As a result of this negative body image, teens may try to alter their bodies, both internally and externally. Sometimes they may even endanger their lives.

Why are the pressures to be perfect so intense for teens? What exactly are the factors that influence our body image? What harm can be done to our health by altering our bodies? And most important, what can we do to prevent ourselves from being trapped in a syndrome of self-hatred?

2

Influences on Image: Societal, Peer, and Media Pressures

"I'd like to look like Cindy Crawford," says Rosie, age thirteen.

....

"I'd like to look like Sylvester Stallone," says Joel, age thirteen.

....

"I would like to be tiny but skinny—like 100 pounds instead of 106, so I can fit into clothes that are cool," says Kelly, age fifteen.

....

"If I could look like someone else, I'd like to look like my friend, because he looks cooler," says Adam, age thirteen.

....

What makes a person want to look thinner, taller, cooler? When we examine all the influences on our body image, we find a complex mix of factors. And although the greatest influences may be messages from the outside, it is really the way we interpret those messages that determines whether or not we have a positive or negative body image. Self-esteem, life experiences, expectations from society, and cultural ideals and values all play a part in how we see ourselves.

Self-esteem and Body Image

Self-esteem and one's body image have a very close relationship. Sometimes they're so close, in fact, that it's hard to separate the two ideas. Body image is concerned with feelings about one's physical self, whereas self-esteem has to do with feelings about one's overall sense of personal value and worth. Positive self-esteem is a feeling of respect for and belief in oneself. Poor self-esteem is the lack of respect for and belief in oneself.

It is interesting to note that people with high self-esteem usually feel good about their bodies, and those with low self-esteem are often unhappy with the way they look. Some studies suggest that girls and women experience a closer link between high self-esteem and a positive body image than boys and men do. This is probably the result of so many centuries of valuing a woman only for her attractiveness and ability to bear children (both physical attributes). A male's body image has always been tied not only to his actual appearance but to his body's effectiveness— his strength, his coordination, his endurance.

Experts who have studied behavior have learned that certain conditions—apart from a positive body image—increase a person's level of self-esteem. One important condition is having a sense of being connected, or belonging, to people, places, or groups that give a person satisfaction or pleasure. Another condition is experiencing a sense of being unique, of feeling that one has special qualities, and that these special qualities are appreciated or recognized. Other important conditions are feeling a sense of power or control over one's own life and having positive role models.[1] All these conditions make a person feel valued, and give that person a special and meaningful place in the world.

Nevertheless, while these other factors contribute to one's overall sense of worth, perhaps none is more important than a positive body image. Because humans are essentially social beings, the messages we get from society are all-important in determining how we fit in and measure up. Currently, the messages from society are loud and clear in announcing just how much appearance counts.

Parents, Coaches, and Teachers

Parents are the first messengers. They give young people their earliest and most consistent messages about their worth as individuals. It makes a difference what qualities one's parents value in a person and how much they emphasize appearance. Parents can do serious harm to a child's fragile self-image by criticizing the child's overall appearance—or a specific body trait. Likewise, overpraising a child's physical appearance or one specific trait can do equal harm, and cause the child to link all his or her feelings of value with appearance in general or with that one overpraised feature.

Parents can play an important role in helping a child develop a positive body image by teaching acceptance and the value of diversity. Not everyone is tall. Not everyone is thin. Not everyone has breasts like the models in the *Victoria's Secret* catalog, legs like Julia Roberts, or muscles like Arnold Schwarzenegger. Not everyone is supposed to. Parents who promote a healthy body image in their children will point this out.

Parents are the first teachers. They give children their earliest messages about their worth as individuals.

Dusty, a twelve-year-old shorter than most boys his age, said, "My dad is small, too, and it doesn't bother him. He's a happy person. He says you've just got to live with it. I've accepted that I really can't change this. I like my body."[2]

Raina, a successful size fourteen model, told of her struggles to accept her somewhat larger size in spite of the teasing she experienced at school. Raina explained that her mom, of similar size and build, was comfortable with her own image and always told Raina that "having a womanly body is something to be proud of."[3]

Teachers, coaches, religious leaders, and other adult authority figures also have a strong influence on a teen's body image. Under their careful guidance, teens can learn the value of intelligence, teamwork, cooperation, and kindness as qualities that can balance physical shortcomings. Likewise, the influence these people exert over teenagers, if used improperly, can often lead to lifelong insecurities and a pattern of chronic stress.

Hurtful remarks from teachers and relatives can cause considerable pain. Silvia, age twelve, confides, "I can never forget when my third-grade teacher told me I looked like a boy." In a recent survey a fifty-nine-year-old man recalled, "being teased when I was a child made me feel bad about my body for years and years."

In sports, too much emphasis on weight and body build can easily lead to eating disorders, an improper and dangerous use of weights, or the use of anabolic steroids. These problems have become so widespread

Gymnasts and other athletes often risk developing eating disorders. An organization called USA Gymnastics has set up a program to educate coaches about this problem.

and common that organizations like USA Gymnastics are becoming involved. This group's athlete wellness program includes information to educate coaches on detecting and preventing eating disorders in the athletes they train.

Notre Dame cross-country star Joanna Deeter relies on a support system at the university to help her battle an eating disorder. This team includes her coach, Tim Connelly. "We made an agreement that she continue to get help with this problem in order to come out for track," Connelly said. "Joanna now has developed more self-confidence, as well as a proper perspective on running."[4]

Coaches', teachers', and relatives' opinions count a lot. But clearly, the opinions that count the most to teens belong to their peers. Teenagers, whose social relationships are still developing, look to their class-mates for reassurance and acceptance. In addition to seeking the approval of same-sex friends, both girls and boys become preoccupied with what impact they are making on the opposite sex. This puts even more pressure on the need to conform to an ideal standard of appearance.

Girls worry about their weight, the condition of their skin, and the size of their breasts. Boys worry about their height, body hair, muscles, and genitals. Many times a person's idealized body even surpasses the expectations of the opposite sex. Studies have shown that many girls seek a figure even thinner than boys appear to admire.[5] Many professionals blame this distorted female ideal on our modern American culture.

Pop Culture and the Media

Everywhere you look, images of thin, young, beautiful women and toned, muscular men are looking back at you. This idealized image is the symbol of our popular culture. Culture includes all aspects of a civilization—its politics, fashions, arts and crafts, educational goals, and public icons. "Culture is so impacting," says one youth worker. "Culture is our mirror—and not just for youth."[6]

Perhaps the strongest dictator of tastes in our culture is the media. Television, newspapers, magazines, the movies, music videos, and advertisements not only reflect the tastes of the American public, but actually form those tastes. Our greatest cultural expectations about our appearance come primarily from these sources.

Advertisements

"Advertisements sell more than products," says Walt Mueller, director for the Center for Parent/Youth Understanding in Pennsylvania. "They sell image. They sell satisfaction. They sell the teen dream of acceptance, popularity, love, and attention."[7]

By the tenth time you pass a billboard and the thirtieth time you see a commercial on television or an ad in a magazine, you may find the ad's message to be part of your subconscious, like it or not. That is why we associate certain tunes with certain products. It is also why we tend to feel that buying the right product will enhance our homes, our job prospects, our popularity, and our sex appeal.

Even though a woman may not actually buy the product being advertised, the way the product is presented may have a lasting impact on her body image. A large percentage of advertisements promote a negative body image. If a woman doesn't try to improve her appearance, these ads insinuate, she won't get a guy, a friend, or a job, and, in fact, she might not even get noticed.

For guys, the advertisements are constantly saying that besides being muscular, it is important to project a "cool" attitude. The guys in the ads are almost always handsome, well built, and surrounded by beautiful women. This is obviously the formula for male success.

Magazines

The magazines that contain these ads also influence teens with their editorial content—their own feature stories and photo layouts. A 1997 report from the Kaiser Family Foundation and Children Now shows that 37 percent of articles, as well as 80 percent of advertisements in teen magazines focus on appearance.[8] Several recent studies indicate that at least 50 percent of adolescent girls, most of them in middle school, regularly read fashion magazines like *Seventeen* or *Vogue*.[9] Generally, the articles that appear in these magazines relentlessly reinforce the same message about image: Thin is beautiful, sexy is beautiful, and appearance must be beautiful.

Many magazines structure their entire format around this message. Advice is offered on how to

Today, "people want to look like the people in magazines—they don't want to be left out," says Sara, age thirteen.

achieve this ideal image. Typical articles from several popular magazines are titled "Escape Your Shape," "Be a Babe," "Foods for an Amazing Bod," "How Hollywood Stays Thin," and "Diet-Pill Update." A quick survey of a recent supermarket magazine rack revealed no fewer than ten magazines with feature articles on slimming down for summer, increasing one's bust size, or shaping up one's bottom. Even *Prevention* and *Reader's Digest* featured articles on losing weight.

One commentator writes, "It is a genetic impossibility for 90 percent of American women to make their bodies look like the bodies of Miss Americas and fashion models—no matter how much they diet or exercise or how much plastic surgery they have."[10]

Columnist Ellen Goodman adds, "A generation ago, the average model weighed 8 percent less than the average woman. Now she weighs 23 percent less."[11]

Michael Levine, professor of psychology at Kenyon College in Ohio, says,

> To succeed, the "modern woman" must present her "self" in a manner that proclaims control and "fitness": the superwoman should have "buns (and abs) of steel". . . .She should have a slender, taut, "lean and (not too) mean" (but somehow full-breasted) appearance, accomplished by strict adherence to dietary and fitness regimens. . . .[12]

In contrast, most magazines for boys and men focus their editorial features less on appearance and more on activities and hobbies. Although most do have articles on fashion and grooming, more of their editorial content relates to activities and products that capture men's interest: for example, cars *(Road & Track)*, sports *(Sports Illustrated)*, hiking and camping *(Outdoor Life)*, and even cigars *(Cigar Aficionado)*.

Although some of these magazines glorify aspects of masculine behavior that are demeaning to women, most of the articles in the magazines most teenage boys buy *(Surfer, Dirt Bike, Game Pro, Body Boarding)* are about personal achievement, taking risks, rebelling, and overcoming obstacles.

Concerned professionals who regularly treat people whose negative body image has resulted in disturbed behavior have finally called upon magazine editors and other journalists to include more diversity in the shape of the models they choose. Several new magazines published for girls and women offer a different focus. *Mode* is a successful fashion glossy for women size twelve and up. *Blue Jeans*, an alternative magazine with a teen editorial board, accepts no advertising and targets body image. *Empower*, another magazine for girls, features topics such as vegetarianism, teen athletes, and body image issues. It recently ran a story called "I'm Ugly on the Outside but That's the Beauty of It."

Television and the Movies

Perhaps even more than magazines, television is responsible for spreading the most pervasive messages about body image. "Over the course of a typical year, children and adolescents spend more time watching television than in any other activity except sleeping."[13]

"You see all these people on TV, and they look so happy and thin, and they make you feel like you should be that way—not just to feel good, but to get the men/women," comments Paula, age seventeen, a Wisconsin high school student.

Michael Levine points out that cultural norms can change. He says, "We've seen some pretty dramatic changes in attitudes toward behavior. For example, domestic violence, drunk driving, and now cigarette smoking—these have all become unacceptable."[14]

Perhaps in the near future the glorification of one body type will be seen as equally destructive. As

Linda Ellerbee, a television reporter, said in a special *Nickelodeon* presentation on body image, "The Body Trap," "We've come to appreciate the diversity of race. Now, let's appreciate the diversity of size and shape."[15] Television specials like this one can help change the current attitudes about appearance. Featuring actresses and actors with different body types, as well as of different races, also promotes an appreciation of diversity. The popularity of performers like Rosie O'Donnell sends a clear signal to producers that it's okay to feature this diversity. Likewise, the popularity of shows like *Living Single* showed the world that four twentysomething women with "real" bodies could enchant and entertain as well as *Friends*.

Even supermodels with perfect bodies like Tyra Banks know something about "getting real." Banks recently cautioned all women to watch out for the media hype. In an interview in the *Los Angeles Times* she warned,

> . . . When it comes to women looking in magazines, enjoy it, and then put it down, because it's all fantasy and a lot of it is fake. A lot of it is pins and tucks and nips and a lot of retouching, too. I hate it when women look at magazine models and get insecure. They don't know that if they were to see me standing naked with no makeup on, and my hair not done, they would feel a lot more comfortable.[16]

Well, maybe just a little.

3

A Short
History of the
Human Form

According to a national study recently released by the Kaiser Family Foundation and Children Now, in the media as a whole, between 26 and 46 percent of all women are portrayed as "thin" or "very thin."[1] That wasn't always the case. Today's attitudes about beauty have changed drastically from those of the past.

For most of history, a rounded female body was associated with beauty. In paintings from many centuries of Western civilization, the contours of the female form, and ample contours at that, are eagerly celebrated. Round curves and faces, and generous arms and thighs were lovingly

In earlier times, a rounded female body was seen as the ideal of health and beauty. This painting by Renoir celebrates the ample form.

detailed. Thin women may be idealized today, but in earlier times being thin was considered an indication of sickness or poverty.

Men's bodies were also a source of artistic inspiration. Greek and Roman art celebrated the ideal athletic young male—a more natural, as opposed to pumped up, muscular form. Beauty in men and boys was also emphasized during the Renaissance.

By the nineteenth century, however, the beauty of the human body came to be identified mainly with the female form. Men were admired more for their intellect, power, and ability to provide material wealth than for their physiques. At this time, the short, thin man was held in the same regard as today's tall, muscular hunk.[2]

At about the same time in history, women's fashions began to dictate the use of some painful and unnatural body-controlling devices. Although the ideal female body remained round and curvy, along came corsets, bustles, wire hoops, stays, and girdles. These changed the look, but not the essential quantity, of the feminine form. By the 1920s women were seriously playing down their curves, bobbing their hair, and shortening their skirts. Some even bound their chests in an effort to look more boyish. The men, too, tried to appear slim and mysterious, in homage to film stars like Rudolph Valentino.

In the 1930s, female movie stars like Marlene Dietrich looked sophisticated and elegant, and slimness remained the ideal. But feminine curves made a big comeback in the 1940s. World War II pinup girls like Betty Grable and Jane Russell brought back in

In the past, the ideal body was different than it is now. Margaret Gorman of Washington, D.C., was sixteen years old when she won the first Miss America contest in 1921 (it began as a publicity gimmick staged by Atlantic City businessmen).

vogue the fuller-figured woman. Then came the fifties, with more of the same. Marilyn Monroe and Sophia Loren ruled. The popularity of movies spread this well-endowed ideal far and wide and also reinforced the ideal of the tall, dark, handsome leading man. Male beauty had returned to the public eye as a saleable commodity.

When we got to the sixties, everything changed. A British rock band called the Beatles revolutionized not only music, but fashion and hairstyles as well. Growth in the television industry offered new and alternative ideals to those already being promoted in the movies. Two other powerful, sometimes opposite, forces appeared to influence how one should appear. One of these forces was the women's liberation, or feminist, movement. The other was the fashion industry.

The feminist movement encouraged people to accept more than one ideal form and type.

In addition to changing the political landscape, the feminist movement affected ideas about appearance. Women were encouraged to take control of their own bodies. They were also encouraged to accept more than one ideal form. In contrast to past years, diverse racial and ethnic looks were now considered attractive by the fashion mainstream.

However, despite the feminists' acceptance of diversity, the fashion industry had a different impact on how women viewed their bodies. Aided by the popularity of fashion magazines and wider media coverage, a new beauty ideal was promoted, and fashion models were elevated to celebrity status. These new stars set the style of extreme slenderness that has remained in fashion ever since. A British model named Twiggy and her thin, straight figure became the new symbol of womanhood.[3] By the 1970s, teenagers were starving or purging themselves in an effort to achieve the kind of body successful models like Twiggy were parading down the runways and into the fashion advertisements.

Zibby Schwarzman, a college student, wrote in *Seventeen* magazine,

> Perhaps the reason my self-image changed when I gained weight was because of the way women are expected to feel about their bodies. I see thin women in magazines, in movies, on television, and those are the images I aspire to. I've always wished that I could be transported back to the era when being a little chunky was considered fashionable.[4]

Eating Disorders: Serious Problems for Teenagers

Today, our society's obsession with weight has become so widespread and commonplace that even eight- and nine-year-olds talk about it. Worrying about one's weight can lead to unhealthy dieting and even to serious eating disorders.

Over and over, our popular culture tells us that fat is bad and thin is good. But how thin is thin? In 1920, the perfect body was said to belong to popular film star Annette Kellerman who at five feet three inches weighed 130 pounds. In 1989, the perfect body supposedly belonged to *Victoria's Secret* supermodel Stephanie Seymour who at five feet ten

Many of today's models give teenage girls the false impression that a thin figure is the only acceptable body type.

inches weighed 127 pounds. Miss Sweden of 1951 was five feet seven inches and weighed 151 pounds, but Miss Sweden of 1983 was five feet nine inches and weighed 109.[1] Today, supermodel Kate Moss, widely admired by teenage girls everywhere, is five feet seven inches and weighs only 100 pounds.[2]

Weight has always been a greater issue for girls than for boys, because girls have always been more exclusively prized for and defined by their physical characteristics. For boys, appearance has been simply one aspect, or part, of who they are. While it's cool to look fit, it's just as cool to be athletic or funny. However, the traditionally relaxed male outlook on weight may be changing. Now, many boys are putting a premium on slenderness, and the number of male eating disorders, unheard of until a few years ago, is growing. In addition, the intense, competitive nature of modern sports adds to the pressures many boys are experiencing. Sports such as wrestling, where being a few pounds too heavy can disqualify you from a match, demand that participants occasionally starve themselves. Such strict weight regulations may eventually push a boy toward an eating disorder.[3]

Sudden Changes

Adolescence means one thing for boys and another for girls. As boys mature, they develop deeper voices, broader shoulders, more muscular bodies, and facial hair. In a way, they are developing naturally into the cultural ideal. The natural maturation of girls,

Some sports like wrestling demand that participants maintain strict weight standards. This pressure may eventually push a person toward an eating disorder.

however, is leading them away from the cultural ideal. Suddenly their lean, straight, slim-limbed bodies are developing curves and pockets of fat. Furthermore, with the onset of menstruation, girls are having to cope with fluctuating hormones and their accompanying mood swings and skin eruptions. Everything is happening at once and quite quickly.

Often, teenage girls have a hard time balancing their emotions. They haven't yet acquired the maturity or the experience to handle the sudden changes and the outside pressures. When they look around for reassurance and acceptance of their new body forms, they see signs everywhere that they need to conform to the old ideal standard.

David M. Garner, director of the Toledo Center for Eating Disorders in Ohio writes,

> Girls today not only have more weight concerns when they're young, they also lack buffers to protect their psyches. Kids don't know themselves well and have not yet developed many competencies to draw on. It's easier for them to look outside themselves to discover who they are—and [they] find themselves lacking."[4]

Dieting

Dieting has come to be America's national pastime. The dieting industry is estimated to be worth more than $30 billion a year.[5] According to an article in *Seventeen* magazine, nearly half of all American women of normal weight are on diets.

Among teenagers, dieting is even more widespread. Not only that, but dieting practices involving more than a simple restriction of calories are often used to control weight in teenagers. These dieting practices include bingeing, or eating uncontrollably, then purging, or voluntarily ridding oneself of the food just eaten. A 1997 Commonwealth Fund survey found that up to 25 percent of adolescents (90 percent of them girls) regularly purge themselves to control their weight.[6]

Dieting can be hazardous to your health, especially when you are young. Because young bodies are still growing and developing, they need calcium for the formation of strong bones and teeth, as well as many other nutrients. They also need enough fat so that their nervous systems can develop properly.

Sex hormones are stored in fatty tissue. Therefore, low fat reserves in women are sometimes linked with a weak level of estrogen, low levels of other important sex hormones, and inactive ovaries. Underweight women also double their risk of having low-birth weight babies.

From birth until puberty, girls of all cultures have 10 to 15 percent more fat in their bodies than boys. Then, at puberty, the male fat-to-muscle ratio decreases, and the female ratio increases. This increased fat ratio in adolescent girls is normal and is nature's way of preparing their bodies for sexual maturation and fertility. By the age of twenty, a healthy female has an average of 28.7 percent body fat. By middle age, women of all cultures have approximately 38 percent body fat. Weight gain with increased age is normal for both sexes.[7]

Teenage girls need at least twenty-two hundred calories a day (some put the minimum at three thousand), and, while the girls are growing, 30 percent or more of these calories should come from fat sources.[8] It is normal for teenage girls to store anywhere from 20 to 25 percent of their body weight as fat, compared to only 14 percent for boys.[9] When body fat levels in teenage girls drop below 5 to 10 percent, the girls put themselves at risk for amenorrhea (cessation of menstruation), as well as for decreased bone mass, the low levels of sex hormones just mentioned, and many other serious health problems.

Adolescent girls who diet excessively may also be programming their bodies for a lifetime battle with weight. Judith Rodin, a psychologist, writes that there is evidence to prove that dieting during adolescence, the time when sex hormone levels are being established and regulated, interferes with the regulation of normal body weight in the future.[10]

Another shocking fact is that, according to the

"How to Lose Weight" articles in teen magazines and the great variety of diet products available can give girls the message that dieting is a necessary part of growing up as a woman.

National Institutes of Health, diets often don't work. A five-year study conducted by Dr. Thomas Wadden at the University of Pennsylvania showed that 98 percent of all dieters regain their previous weight within five years.[11] Ironically, strict dieting may actually promote weight gain, researchers say. As a way of protecting itself against severe caloric restriction, the body lowers its basal metabolic rate (the rate at which the body burns calories to produce energy for vital bodily processes) in an effort to save calories. As a result of a lower, or slower, metabolism, the body now burns calories at a slower rate, and the body requires less calories than it used to in order to gain the same amount of weight.

"Yo-yo" dieting—the cycle of dieting, losing weight, then regaining the weight and dieting again—can increase the risk of death from heart disease by as much as 70 percent.[12] Liquid protein diets may also lead to heart trouble, or even sudden death. The ingredients in many diet pills have caused much national controversy, and are linked with side effects ranging from heart seizure to psychoses. For these reasons it is important for people to diet under the supervision of a doctor or professional nutritionist.

These professionals are also trained to avoid an individual's tendency to focus on pounds, rather than on overall body type. Most dieters intent on losing weight ignore the fact that people have different builds. In their quest for the "perfect weight," they forget that a person may be fit and still weigh more than another person of the same height. Heredity plays a significant role in both body size and shape and in metabolic rate. Many health professionals are suggesting a new, health-centered approach to weight control, stressing the need to be healthy instead of a particular size.

Yet despite the national obsession with dieting, the latest report from government surveys shows that more Americans than ever are overweight. Kelly Brownell, a psychologist at Yale University, blames this trend on the "toxic food environment with easily available, high-fat good-tasting foods . . . and the decline in physical exercise."[13] An article in the *Los Angeles Times* offers the shocking statistic that 50 percent of thirteen- to nineteen-year-olds in the United States today do not engage in any strenuous physical activity.[14]

Television may be partially responsible. Watching it reduces the amount of time a person might otherwise spend pursuing physical activity. In addition, its advertisements tend to promote the consumption of high-fat, nutritionally shallow foods. To make matters worse, at the same time that television, video and computer games, and music videos continue to fill more of a child's free time, physical education programs in some schools are being cut or seriously reduced.

Exercise is a good alternative to dieting. Exercise gets the body doing what it was designed to do, and stresses function over appearance. In addition, aerobic exercise increases the body's metabolic rate, which keeps the body processes working efficiently to burn off calories. Exercise can reinforce healthier eating habits and regulate appetite. It has also been

Exercise is a healthy alternative to dieting. It increases the body's efficiency in burning calories and naturally combats anxiety and depression.

shown to combat anxiety, depression, and mood swings, which are often associated with weight gain. However, as with all other good things in life, moderation is the key. In addition to physical damage such as injuries or the cessation of menstruation in women, too much exercise can actually cause the same ironic problems as stringent dieting, making it harder to keep weight off in the long run.

Although dieting can cause long-term health problems, it's hard for a teen to worry about something that might happen far into the future. A teenage girl who begins a diet, limiting herself to five hundred to one thousand calories a day, doesn't plan on developing an eating disorder. Unfortunately, however, that's exactly how most girls with eating disorders begin their self-imposed pain.

Eating Disorders

> I was in so much pain, I didn't think I had any other options. I was caught in this eating disorder and just watching myself slowly committing suicide. —*former anorexic*[15]

An eating disorder is considered a compulsion. That means someone who has one is no longer able to make choices about his or her behavior. The behavior is out of one's control. The person has an irresistible impulse to act, regardless of how illogical the action may be. With an eating disorder, a person is unable to stop oneself from using food as a means to try to satisfy an emotional need.

Although an eating disorder is a compulsive behavior toward food, it isn't so much about the food itself as it is about psychological factors like lacking self-esteem or feeling depressed. Biological and genetic factors, social conditions, and family background all play a part. The seeds for an eating disorder are often sown early in childhood. Then, when puberty brings the teenager face-to-face with unpleasing physical changes and the emotional turmoil of adolescence, the combination of these pressures, added to the cultural emphasis on thinness, may trigger an eating disorder.

The three most common eating disorders are anorexia nervosa, bulimia nervosa, and compulsive overeating. Anorexia nervosa is essentially self-starvation. Bulimia is a disorder in which a person eats a large amount of food (bingeing) and then rids the body of that food (purging) before it can be absorbed. A person who is bulimic purges either by inducing vomiting or by using laxatives or diuretics (water pills).

Although specialists are seeing more males with these disorders, 90 to 95 percent of anorexics and bulimics are women. Anorexia and bulimia are not mutually exclusive. Approximately half of all persons who have anorexia nervosa also suffer from bulimia nervosa, and many patients with bulimia nervosa have "anorectic" attitudes and periods of anorectic behavior. A third disorder, compulsive overeating, happens when a person turns to food as a way of trying to cope with, avoid, or make up for the stresses in life.

Anorexia Nervosa

Anorexia affects mainly girls between the ages of fourteen and eighteen, although preteens are also at risk. Anorexics have an intense fear of becoming fat, so much so that they actually starve themselves. Often they weigh as little as eighty to one hundred pounds. Even then, these people may sometimes see themselves as fat. As one expert puts it, they have a "disturbance in body image of delusional proportions."[16] Many anorexics overexercise and use diet pills as well. If they continue in this mode of behavior, they are at great risk of dying from suicide, heart attack, or starvation. Because they eat so little, it might be surprising to learn that anorexics have an obsession with food. Food is rarely out of their thoughts. An anorexic may limit herself to eating only "safe" foods, usually those low in calories or fat. In addition she may cut up food into very small pieces, spend more time playing with the food than eating it, or buy, prepare, and cook food only for others. At the same time an anorexic develops one or more of these obsessive relationships with her food, she is always hungry.

Since she spends most of her time thinking about food, figuring out how to avoid eating, and trying to stave off the pangs of hunger, the anorexic has little time to think about anything else. Her day is ruled by

People who suffer from anorexia nervosa have compulsive rituals about food. These rituals, such as cutting food into small pieces, can rule their lives.

obsessive-compulsive rituals. In addition, the lack of food affects her mental functions. More than ever, she experiences feelings of inferiority about her intelligence, personality, and appearance and is constantly preoccupied with the way she looks. She sees herself as fat and is afraid others will become skinnier than she is. Since a typical person with this illness is feeling a general lack of control over her life, she tries to control the only area she thinks she can—her body. This gives her a sense of power.

However, warns Carolyn Costin of the Eating Disorder Center of California in Malibu, this type of person really has a phobia about control as well as appearance. Costin explains: "There is a huge fear of letting go and losing control. For example, a person with anorexia nervosa who refuses to eat a cookie is worried about the calories, but underneath this is the greater fear of breaking her rule and then losing control. One cookie may lead to another and another and who knows what else."[17]

Anorexia nervosa has the highest death rate of any psychiatric illness—approximately 5 percent of all individuals with this disorder die. These fatalities can be caused by a number of physical factors, including electrolyte imbalance, heart failure, or abnormalities in the electrical conduction through the heart. In addition to life-threatening complications, the illness produces other effects, involving nearly every organ in the body.[18] Some other physical changes it causes include constantly feeling cold (the body has lost the fat and muscle it needs to keep warm); vacant, hollow eyes; protruding bones and shrinking skin around them; loss of hair on the head while fine hair grows on other parts of the body for warmth; brittle, dry hair and fingernails; amenorrhea (cessation of the menstrual cycle), which can lead to an irreversible loss of bone mass; stunted growth, resulting in permanent short stature; and anemia.[19]

Bulimia Nervosa

Bulimia nervosa is another eating disorder that can be life-threatening. Bulimia and anorexia have many of the same symptoms. Both disorders involve an obsession with food and with staying thin. Instead of starving herself like the anorexic, the bulimic gets an uncontrollable urge to binge (eat a large amount of food in a short period of time) and then a desire to purge this food from her body.

Bulimia usually develops between the ages of fifteen and twenty-four. Like anorexia, this disorder affects mostly females. However, unlike an anorexic, a bulimic does not usually look extremely thin—her weight is usually within the normal range for her height and size, but it tends to go up and down a lot because of all the bingeing and purging. Fearing that she won't be able to control her urge to binge or purge, a bulimic may often avoid social situations and isolate herself from others.

The bulimic spends a lot of time, energy, and money on food. She becomes very secretive, and puts much effort into thinking about and planning the next binge and setting aside specific times to binge.

People with the eating disorder called bulimia often try to hide their behavior, which includes bingeing and purging. Constantly worrying about where to get rid of the food they've eaten greatly limits their social lives.

She steals food or hoards it in secret places, such as under the bed or in closets.

Like anorexics, bulimics are not happy with their body image. They perceive themselves as fat or overweight. They, too, usually start out dieting. However, in response to anxiety and other emotions, they wind up giving in to their impulses and cravings for food and go on a binge. During a binge a person with bulimia may eat between three thousand and seven thousand calories, often in less than a few hours. Depression, boredom, or anger can trigger a binge. The actual eating process during a binge is almost robotlike—the impulse is to eat until no food is left, or until the stomach hurts from so much eating. Then the bulimic experiences a sense of guilt, and the fear that she will gain weight. So she gets rid of the food by inducing vomiting or taking pills that cause diarrhea. Then after purging she may turn to extreme exercise or another strict diet, which lasts until the next binge.

This compulsive behavior exacts a big price from the bulimic's body. Some of the negative effects of bulimia are the onset of tooth decay from prolonged contact with stomach acids during vomiting; radically fluctuating weight loss and gain; irregular menstrual periods; a puffy, swollen complexion; periods of dizziness and blackouts; constant upset stomach; constipation; sore throat; and damage to vital organs, such as the liver and kidneys. In addition, dehydration from loss of body fluids can result in an electrolyte imbalance, which, in turn, can lead to cardiac arrhythmias (irregular heartbeats) and eventually to heart damage, even to heart failure and death.[20]

Compulsive Overeating

Compulsive overeating happens when a person turns to food as a way of trying to cope with, avoid, or compensate for the insecurities of life. Compulsive overeaters tend to eat in response to stress. This is an eating disorder from which boys also suffer. Teens who are caught in this pattern often eat constantly, becoming less active or sluggish. When weight gain becomes noticeable, the teen will often go on a diet, then regain the weight, then go on another diet. As with the other two eating disorders, teens tend to hide food and obsess about it. All their energies are concentrated on thinking about food.

Girls who might not be ready for the pressures of dating or boys who might feel unequal to the task of succeeding at sports or with girls may choose to remove themselves from the competitive arena in this way. Food is also comforting when a person is feeling lonely and isolated. Another cause of compulsive overeating might be rebellion. For some teenagers, being fat is a statement of their refusal to conform.[21]

Causes of Eating Disorders

All teenagers are subject to the same pressures from our culture. Why do some successfully ignore or bypass these pressures, and others develop eating disorders? No one can answer that question completely. "It's like a jigsaw puzzle with a lot of pieces," says Carolyn Costin, "I think there's a genetic predisposition. It's psychological and cultural—it's a combination of things."[22] Since each person struggling with a disorder is unique, the following characteristics won't apply in every case. However, specialists have observed some basic common similarities among teenagers who develop eating disorders:

1. low self-esteem

2. social insecurity

3. problems with intimacy

4. problems with control

5. social pressures to conform
   to an ideal body type

6. depression and anxiety

We've already seen that low self-esteem can result in a negative body image, which, in turn, makes a person more vulnerable to other messages he or she may receive. People with eating disorders also feel insecure socially—they might be high achievers, but they are constantly afraid that their "real selves" may slip out and be revealed as laughable or worthless. They are afraid to let others see them as they really are, and they feel safe only if others keep their distance. Depression and anxiety also often go hand in hand with eating disorders—75 percent of bulimics may experience major depression, perhaps as a result of their self-imposed isolation and inability to form and maintain relationships.[23]

Recent studies have indicated that there may also be physical causes as well as psychological ones. Carolyn Costin has reported that there is some abnormality in the brain-wave patterns of girls with serious eating disorders. Indications are that this abnormality existed before the eating-disordered behavior began. However, Costin pointed out that she felt the reason the brain-wave abnormality manifested itself in an eating disorder instead of some other fashion "has everything to do with our culture."[24] One study showed that women with anorexia had unusual brain secretions of a hormone called vasopressin, which regulates the body's water balance, perhaps causing ordinary dieting to turn into compulsive starvation. Another study found that people with anorexia are physically addicted to the dieting process.[25]

A person with an eating disorder needs help. It is a problem that is difficult to solve alone. Often teens are not even able to admit they have the problem. Most teens with eating disorders either deny them completely or are terrified they are unable to stop their own obsessive behavior.

If you think that you have an eating disorder or are spending most of your time worrying about food and whether or not you are gaining weight, then talking to someone about it is a good idea. Once the compulsive behavior has taken hold, you will need help to break that hold—and the earlier you seek help, the better. Sometimes, parents don't realize the seriousness of an eating compulsion until something dramatic happens, but once they are made aware of what you are going through, they will want to help you. School counselors can refer you to someone who can provide the resources you need to overcome this problem. Usually, teens with eating disorders are treated by a team, including a therapist, a nutritionist, and a family physician—each of whom should be specially trained to work with eating-disordered behavior.

In addition, many hospitals sponsor programs that treat eating disorders. Other resources, like hot-lines and web sites, provide places where teens can get help. These are listed in the back of the book under "Resources."

Although eating disorders affect both sexes, it is most often the girls who struggle with excessive diet-ing, anorexia, and bulimia. Boys have their own struggles. For them, as well as for girls, society offers up an almost equally unattainable ideal. While the girls are worrying about being too heavy, many boys are despairing at not being heavy enough, or tall enough, or man enough. They, too, seek solutions to achieve a perfect body image. These solutions can be just as harmful as eating disorders.

5

Fears, Steroids, and Muscle Mania

Ask a teenage boy how he feels about his body image and he might echo Trent, age seventeen: "I don't answer any questions with the word 'feeling' in it." Boys don't talk much about issues related to their appearance. However, boys still have body image concerns. Many adolescent males worry about whether they are too short or small, whether their physical development is normal, or whether they have large enough muscles.

Just like teenage girls, boys face cultural pressures to conform to an unrealistic ideal body type. The modern cultural emphasis on bodybuilding has produced

54

more men and boys with a negative body image. In *Psychology Today*'s 1997 body image survey, 41 percent of young men ages thirteen to nineteen said they were dissatisfied with their appearance.[1]

Concerns About Height

Height is probably the major body image concern for male adolescents. One boy who was small for his age talked about the names he was commonly called by others. "Shorty," "shrimp," and "chicken wing" were just a few of them. Whether this boy will remain short all his life depends on several factors, including heredity. If he has short parents and is far along in his physical development, the chances are he will be shorter than average. If the males in his family are late bloomers and his parents are tall, he may be, too.

For a boy who is worried about his stature, a physical exam can help determine his developmental stage and whether there are any physical problems that need to be addressed. For those who suffer a great deal because of shortness and delayed puberty, hormonal treatment is a possible option. However, there are side effects, not all of which are known. In fact, artificially accelerating the growth process may later cause the boy to be shorter than he would have been without the therapy.[2]

For most boys, a better way to deal with height insecurities is to focus on other, different areas that a person does have control over. Developing social skills, an outgoing personality, and a positive attitude can go a long way in creating self-esteem.

Guys can face pressure to be a superjock or an exaggerated macho superhero like Rambo. At the same time, they're worrying about how tall they'll be in high school.

Jose, a California junior high school student who is short, says he admires his brother because "he ain't big or tall, but he is strong and crazy."

Not everyone is meant to be a basketball or football star. Sports in which size isn't so important are increasingly popular as well as financially rewarding. Soccer, gymnastics, wrestling, diving, surfing, golf, skating, and skateboarding are some sports that provide an opportunity to excel regardless of size. In some cases, being short can even be a plus. For example, most competitive inline skaters are of below-average height. Raphael Sandoz, a 1997 Extreme Games winner, is five feet three inches. Surfers who are short have an advantage, because a lower center of gravity enables them to balance and make the quick turns necessary to adjust to a wave. They also fit better "in the tube" that forms under the crest of a wave as it's breaking.

Physical Development—What's Normal?

Like the girls, teenage boys compare themselves to their peers to evaluate whether or not they are normal. Since puberty doesn't arrive at the same time for everyone, boys of the same age can be worlds apart, hormonally speaking. One fourteen-year-old named Andy is under five feet tall, smooth-cheeked, and high-voiced. His friend Link, also fourteen, is pushing six feet, beginning to grow a mustache, and speaks in a deep, booming baritone. Andy avoids situations where physical comparisons are made.

Perhaps the most devastating comparison gets made in the boys' locker room, or during PE showers. Boys are routinely subjected to teasing about the size and appearance of their genitals, particularly late bloomers. These young men, already self-conscious and insecure, can suffer severe emotional stress from this experience. Ironically, as nudity in the movies and on TV becomes more common, boys seem to be more sensitive than ever about exposing their bodies in front of other males. Perhaps now there are just too many perfect bodies to compare oneself with.

Whatever the reason, fewer and fewer kids are showering in PE classes. A physical education department chair and varsity football coach at Venice High School says fear of showers there isn't new. "In the last ten years almost no one showers. Embarrassment is part of it. Our football guys go in there with their girdles and pads on to shower. Most of them just put on deodorant and go to their parties. We finally stopped handing out towels."[3] A *Los Angeles Times* reporter interviewed a high school student on this subject. A tall and skinny fifteen-year-old, the boy admitted he'd only be subjecting himself to mockery if he took a shower in front of the other guys. He said, "I have PE second period, so I have to like load on the Right Guard and hope it lasts me," says the teen, who asked that his name not be used. "Don't even say what color hair I have. . . . I'm sort of a geek anyway, so I don't need any more hassles."[4]

Speed, stamina, and dexterity, not necessarily size, count in sports like soccer.

Muscles and Anabolic Steroids

For many teenage boys, weight is also an issue. In contrast to the girls, boys want to put on more weight rather than take it off. Stan, seventeen, is on a swim team. "You don't know what it's like to stand up there on the block in your red Speedo," he said, "and know that everyone is counting your ribs."

Not every guy can be built like a weightlifter, but many try. For some, working out just isn't enough. This has led to an alarming increase in the number of young men willing to change their bodies through the use of drugs such as anabolic steroids. Studies indicate that as many as two hundred fifty thousand American teens may be trying to improve their body image this way.[5] Although the majority use these drugs to make themselves bigger, tougher, and meaner on the athletic field, some just want to look good on the beach. As Adam, thirteen, says, "[I want] to have a six-pack, you know, be cut [abdominal muscles defined or 'cut' to look like a six-pack of aluminum cans]."

According to one source, the widespread male fascination with "being cut" compares to the widespread desire of women to be thin. Dr. Gary Wadler, who won a 1993 International Olympic Committee prize for his work on drugs and sports, compares steroid takers to victims of eating disorders like anorexia and bulimia. "One is the relentless pursuit of bigness, the other is the relentless pursuit of thinness," he says. "They're polar aspects of the same problem." One result of this male pursuit of bigness may be a "reverse anorexia," as men become compulsive exercisers or abusers of steroids in trying to attain an otherwise unattainable ideal body type.[6]

One teenage boy explained the current fascination with "pumping up": "[Guys] want to look good for the girls, but also so they won't be teased (or worse) by other guys." Adds anthropologist and author David Gilmore, "Boys are beaten up if they don't measure up. To be masculine requires a certain musculature."[7]

Anabolic Steroid Abuse

Anabolic steroids, popularly referred to as "steroids," are drugs that can be taken orally or injected. They are synthetic derivatives of the hormone testosterone, which is responsible for androgenic (masculinizing) and anabolic (tissue building) characteristics. These synthetic drugs can increase body weight (especially lean body weight) and, in combination with high-intensity weight training, can increase muscle strength by unnaturally accelerating the process of building muscle. They may also lead to increased strength, not only by increasing muscle gain but by increasing the athlete's aggressiveness, producing euphoria, or decreasing the athlete's sense of fatigue during training.

Steroid use has continued to rise to a degree many doctors call alarming. Dr. Steven Anderson, chairman of the American Academy of Pediatrics' Committee on Sports Medicine and Fitness, says that a conservative estimate of the number of steroid users in the United States is between 2 and 5 percent of all those involved in athletics. Some claim the figure is as high as 11 percent. Steroid use is clearly more common among males, although the number of females involved in this practice is rising as girls in some competitive sports face the same pressures as boys to increase their strength, endurance, and aggressiveness. A Massachusetts study of three thousand high school students found that 5.7 percent of boys reported using steroids, as opposed to 1.7 percent of girls.[8]

Why has steroid use shown such an increase? There can be several reasons, including the accelerated pressures to succeed in athletics, a growing interest in bodybuilding, and the current cultural emphasis on the lean, muscular body.

Nonmedical use of anabolic steroids first began in the 1950s among weight lifters and other "strength" athletes, in the hope of gaining strength and bulk beyond what could naturally be achieved by training and diet alone. Now, in spite of being illegal, steroid use has spread to other parts of the population, including teens.

Dr. Anderson states, "It's important to note that steroid use is not just limited to athletes or males. Athletes may feel it is necessary to take steroids to perform well. Non-athletes take them just to bulk up—to match a more desirable body type."

Teenagers offer additional reasons why the use of steroids seems appealing. Junior high and high school can be a painful experience for boys who are late bloomers. Sometimes, these boys turn to steroids to try and control their fate—including their height and weight. They become willing to try anything that promises to relieve the cause of their pain. At their age, the concept of long-term risk-taking is glamorous, if anything, and the consequences of one's behavior are rarely considered.

Athletic Use of Steroids

Athletes receive a message to perform whatever the cost. The temptation for athletes to use steroids comes from many sources, including the demands of the sport itself, particularly in sports such as football, weight lifting and some track events. Many coaches and even parents contribute to the pressures to achieve a lean body mass, muscles, and athletic superiority. Dr. Anderson reveals that this pressure is more common than might be expected: "A parent might say, my kid needs to take steroids so he can get a scholarship to play football in college."[9] Sometimes, this pressure motivates an athlete to turn to steroids for an extra edge in achieving that superior performance. However, although steroids may work in the short term, there is a price to be paid. Experts talk about some of the health risks that come with taking steroids.

Steroid Risks

"While there's a lot of junk sold to athletes that does no good at all, it's the junk that does do good that worries professionals," says one expert.[10] One of the difficulties in combatting the use of steroids is that in fact these drugs do promote muscle growth. In addition, many of the problems that result from their use take time to develop. So it's hard to convince some teens that steroids are really dangerous. This attitude is reflected in the comment of Stephen, age fifteen, of Nevada: "If you don't use them [steroids] for more than a year, it's not going to be that bad."

Many teenage boys use steroids, hoping to look more like this bodybuilder.

Dr. Anderson admits,

[Although] there are long-term risks of malignancies, and heart or liver problems from taking steroids, scare tactics don't really work. I think it's better to be honest about the fact that [steroids] do lead to gains in strength over the short-term—when taken in adequate doses. (You can't just sprinkle steroids on your Wheaties and expect to gain lean body mass.) However, people also need to know about the more common physical side effects. These include testicular atrophy [decrease in the size or development of the testicles] along with a decrease in sperm count, acne—which can be pretty severe—baldness—irreversible—and sometimes male breast development as well.[11]

Another irreversible effect of steroid use can be overall stunted growth. Anabolic steroid withdrawal and dependency disorders have also been reported, including depression and anxiety, irritability, insomnia, hot flashes, sweats, chills, and anorexia.[12]

Aggressive and violent behaviors have also been linked to steroid use. "There are definitely psychological and emotional effects from taking steroids," Dr. Anderson points out.

> A direct effect of the hormone is that people may become more aggressive. In fact, one of the theories of the benefits of the steroid was that it only worked because people were more aggressive and they trained harder and got the benefits from the harder training.[13]

Irritability and aggressive behavior can result in what are popularly known as "roid rages."

Risk-taking behavior is also often associated with steroid use. Taking steroids is thought to embolden a user, and he may be more likely to drive after drinking alcohol or to use drugs like cocaine.

Because the use of steroids is illegal, most users generally avoid checking in with their doctors to monitor for side effects. Furthermore, many serious side effects, such as liver damage, may not show up initially. However, steroids do have a cumulative effect on the body.

A track athlete had started to take the drugs, hoping to drop a second or two off his hurdle time, but had second thoughts and consulted his doctor. The doctor explained,

> Before talking to him about the possible effects of steroid use—I doubt if it would have any effect on [his running] speed—I took a blood sample for tests and to measure the lipid [fat] level in the blood. As I drew the athlete's blood, a pale, pink, foamy substance came up into the tube. It looked like a strawberry milkshake, there was so much fat in it. I mean, it was off the scale in terms of lipid content.

The doctor recalled, "I didn't even have to say anything else. He just couldn't believe it—it was very dramatic."[14]

Despite dramatic evidence of the physical dangers, teens are not easily dissuaded from using the drugs. In fact, other issues may have a greater bearing on a teenager's decision to use or not use steroids. "We should give kids more credit for ethical and moral standards," Dr. Anderson says.

> We need to talk about the body as a temple that needs to be protected, but we also need to talk about what's right and what's fair—that achieving something artificially doesn't have the same value as achieving it through effort. There are some great athletes who model this attitude. For example, Edwin Moses, the former Olympic hurdler, said that if he had to use steroids to win a medal, then he wouldn't want it.[15]

Many young athletes echo Moses' attitude. Hudson, a Nebraska teen, says,

> It isn't worth it to hurt your body just to impress people. If what you are doing makes it so that you have to take them [steroids] to do the activity, I would suggest that you check your priorities and either stop using steroids and work out with weights, or take up the activity at a scale that doesn't require using drugs.

Argenis, a thirteen-year-old from California comments: "I don't think it's necessary. All I do is work out and it works and it makes me feel good. Drugs are not a necessary part of my life." Jess, age sixteen, from Wisconsin adds: "I think that any real athlete who is devoted to their sport should be willing to put in the time and effort to increase their actual muscle strength. Anyone who takes steroids is, in my opinion, a disgrace to sports and hard-working, devoted athletes."

Steroids promise a lot—muscles, strength, and endurance. Unfortunately, there's a terrible price to pay. Both your health and your ultimate self-esteem can be seriously compromised. "If you want muscles, you should work for them," says Patty, sixteen. "Steroids are the easy way out."

Boys who struggle with body image problems involving muscularity, height, or physical development should be encouraged to talk about their doubts and fears. Perhaps, if males were more open about their fears and insecurities, it would be possible to change the way our culture perceives both male and female ideals. If more teenage boys admitted how they suffered from a negative body image, perhaps physical diversity would become more accepted. Then boys, as well as girls, would be freer to help each other develop all the aspects of who they are.

While many teens turn to eating disorders and the abuse of drugs like steroids, others turn to different methods to change their bodies. Some of these methods are designed to upset the cultural ideal and separate the teen from society's "norm." Some of the methods are just another, new way to enhance their body image and fit in with their peers. Many of these methods of body modification, rare or unheard of in the past, are now increasingly part of our mainstream culture.

6

Cosmetic Surgery, Tattooing, and Body Piercing

When she set out to achieve her ideal body, Cindy Jackson had a particular body in mind: Barbie's. It didn't matter to her that Barbie is not a real person, but a doll whose dimensions are impossible for a human to achieve. One expert said you'd have to be six feet seven inches tall, weigh one hundred twenty pounds and have a number of ribs removed to duplicate Barbie's proportions. Cindy Jackson, however, remains dedicated to her pursuit. After twenty different surgeries, she still isn't done trying to turn herself into "the contemporary Western feminine ideal."[1]

Not many people tinker with their

69

bodies to this degree. However, the modern perception of the body as an object to improve and embellish has led to the popularity of cosmetic surgery and body modification practices, such as tattooing or piercing.

Psychologist Judith Rodin explains that today one's face and body are regarded as a "mobile billboard" upon which to advertise who one is.[2] Marc Lappé, director of the nonprofit Center for Ethics and Toxic Substances in Gualala, California, calls the skin, as well as the face and body, the "new battleground for defining the self." This is because skin is the "single most visible image we project to the outside world."[3] Some psychologists explain the current focus on changing and modifying the body as a way to protect or draw attention away from what's inside—the true self.

Cosmetic Surgery

Cosmetic surgery is a branch of plastic surgery. The latter gets its name from the Greek word *plastikos* meaning "to mold or shape." Plastic surgery is a specialty that has traditionally been dedicated to reconstructing facial and body defects due to birth disorders, trauma, burns, and disease. One example of traditional plastic surgery would be reconstructing an abnormal body structure like a cleft palate to obtain a more normal appearance.

Cosmetic surgery focuses primarily on reshaping normal, as opposed to abnormal, structures of the body in order to improve the patient's appearance.

An example of cosmetic surgery would be rhinoplasty, or reshaping a normal nose to form the nose that a person would prefer. Rhinoplasty is the most common cosmetic surgery performed on people eighteen years old and younger.

Most teenagers who choose this procedure are girls like Rosie, age thirteen. She says: "I want it because it will make me look just perfect. My stepsister wasn't pretty at all because she had a big honker—like a goose nose. She got plastic surgery and now she's beautiful."

Otoplasty, or ear surgery, to correct ears that stick out or are too big, is the next most common cosmetic surgery for teens. The third most common is breast alteration—augmentation, to make the breasts larger, or reduction, to make them smaller.

Cosmetic surgery is one way people change themselves to improve their body image. It can often help someone who has been handicapped by a particular defect. However, cosmetic surgery is not a magic wand. It can remake your exterior, but it can't change the person you are inside. As with any other surgery, there are risks. Things don't always go as planned. Some people are literally scarred for life. Many others are unhappy with the results.

Others become addicted to the process itself. Cari is a model who has had her eyelids, nose, ears, and breasts done. Yet, Cari still feels that she could improve her appearance. Dr. John Persing, professor and chief of plastic surgery at Yale University Medical School admits this type of person is rare. "If a person does . . . [cosmetic surgery] every six months or so," he says, "usually these people need to work with a psychologist or psychiatrist to understand his or her motivation and to address body image issues that might be at the core of this behavior."[4] Therefore, it is crucial to discuss one's physical and psychological concerns with a plastic surgeon who is both board-certified and affiliated with an accredited hospital.

Although changing the body through cosmetic surgery was once regarded as a solution only for the wealthy few, today it has become a popular option for both men and women. As acceptance of cosmetic surgery has increased, so, too, has the popular acceptance of other body modifications formerly taboo in mainstream culture.

Tattoos—Taboo?

Tattooing, a technique of marking the skin with colored pigment, has been around for at least six thousand years.[5] Crusaders tattooed crucifixes on their bodies as permanent ID tags so that if they were killed, they would be given a Christian burial. New Zealand Maoris, Tahitians, Japanese, South-American Indian tribes, and American Indians also used or continue to use tattoos for religious, tribal, social, or superstitious reasons.

In the past, traditional mainstream Western culture has associated tattooing with atypical lifestyles. Circus performers, sailors, prison inmates, and Hell's Angels were the people one thought of first when considering who wore tattoos. Then, in the 1980s,

Many teenagers consider tattoos and body piercings to be artistic embellishments.

supermodels like Stephanie Seymour and actresses like Julia Roberts publicly exhibited their tattoos on shoulders, ankles, and lower backs. As tattoos have become more acceptable and respectable, "tattoo parlors" have now become "tattoo studios."

Tattoos are made by injecting ink into the lowest layer of living cells of the skin, the basal cell layer, or dermis. An electrically powered, vertically vibrating needle injects the tattoo pigment fifty to three thousand times per minute up to or into the second layer of the skin. Up to fourteen needles may be used to incorporate different colors in the design.[6]

Myrna Armstrong and Kathleen Pace Murphy of Texas Tech University's School of Nursing, recently completed a survey of 2,101 teenagers from seven different states to find out how popular tattooing is among adolescents. "Generally," says Armstrong, "feelings about these practices tend not so much to be regional as to depend on what degree the teenager is into the culture."[7] Thirty percent of the teens surveyed said their tattoos brought disappointment, embarrassment, and low self-esteem when others viewed their tattoos. "I read in the Bible that you're not supposed to do it; now it's a bit difficult for me," said one teen. Another said, "I regret doing it—I hardly let anyone see it."[8] Still, others were happy with the results at this stage of their lives, and about 40 percent felt their tattoos had been helpful in "making them feel unique and special."[9]

Of the 2,101 teens surveyed, 55 percent were interested in getting a tattoo, but only 213, or a little over 10 percent, actually got them. More than half of these were girls. Not surprisingly, Armstrong and Murphy found that teens and adults had differing viewpoints about tattooing. Adolescents see it as an expression of self-identity and body art, whereas adults perceive it as a sign of deviant behavior.[10] "I would like to get a tattoo," says Katie, fifteen, of Nevada, "I think they're part of your creativity."

Health Risks in Tattooing

There are plenty of potential health problems from the tattooing process. "Studio tattoo artists are unlicensed, the ingredients of the pigments are not FDA-approved or standardized, hygiene procedures for equipment are inconsistent, and sanitary inspections of studios are infrequent," says Armstrong.[11]

Dr. Steven Popkow, a Santa Monica, California, physician, specializes in tattoo removal. His opinion is that

> Most tattoo studios use single-use needles, sterilize, and try to clean the equipment, and [they] alternate the equipment between people and use gloves and aseptic techniques to minimize the risk of potential cross-infection, but you never know. If they're in a hurry . . . and they don't have time to wash the [ink] gun between people, they might just change the needle. It can get pretty bloody when they're doing it.[12]

Some of the risks include blood-carried infections. Hepatitis B has been reported to be associated with studio tattooing. In addition, Armstrong notes, "Although the cause is unknown, rare cases of carcinoma have been reported at tattoo sites." A case of leprosy has even been linked to a contaminated tattoo needle.[13] More common health risks include infection of the tattoo site if the procedure is not carried out in a hygienic manner or not kept clean until the skin heals. There are also common skin reactions to the pigments used in tattooing, including allergic reactions and scarring. As a precaution, a person seeking a tattoo should ask for a skin test first to see whether he or she is at risk for an allergic reaction.

Furthermore, all the risks associated with tattooing are increased if amateurs do the tattoos. Without a professional's care, the hygiene is often primitive, the implements may be crude, and the pigments chosen—anything from mascara to soot— may contain harmful agents.

In view of all these risks, it is important to know the right questions to ask before getting a tattoo. A tattoo studio should be glad to show its sterilization area. Ask if the studio uses autoclave technology—a technique that sterilizes by steam and pressure at a temperature hotter than the boiling point of water— to clean its instruments. Are there packaged, sterilized needles, and is each needle used only once, then disposed of in a biohazard container? Are several pairs of new, clean latex gloves used during each procedure? Is leftover ink disposed of—never poured back into the bottle? And finally, is a skin test offered to determine whether any allergic reaction is likely?

Seven states prohibit tattooing for anyone: Connecticut, Florida, Kansas, Massachusetts, Oklahoma, South Carolina, and Vermont. Illinois and North Carolina prohibit the tattooing of minors.

This woman covered over a tattoo of her ex-boyfriend's name with this new design.

Wisconsin, California, Maine, and Texas specifically prohibit tattooing for adolescents without their parents' permission.[14]

Removing Tattoos

Years ago it was impossible to get rid of a tattoo. Today, tattoos can be removed successfully with laser therapy, but the process can be painful, time-consuming, and expensive. People wind up wanting their tattoos removed for various reasons. A common one is to remove a name—like the name of a gang, or an ex-girlfriend or boyfriend.

Dr. Popkow points out, "I have a couple of actors who . . . are spending a lot of money and time now trying to get tattoos off their bodies because they realize it's not good for their careers." He adds, "Those with a gang-related tattoo also might have trouble getting work. Employers don't want to hire somebody who has that stigma on them."

Dr. Popkow has done more than two thousand laser tattoo removals:

> We usually can get 95 percent of the ink off, so from a cosmetic point of view, people are very happy with it. The laser units are expensive, so the treatments are, too. On the average, it costs about three hundred dollars per square inch to remove a tattoo. There is about a 30 to 50 percent fading per treatment, so it's actually about a six-month, six-treatment process to fade a professional tattoo.[15]

Getting a tattoo involves more than a quick trip to a tattoo studio. Perhaps it makes sense to heed the words of Guns & Roses lead singer Axl Rose: "Think and rethink before you ink."[16]

Body Piercing

"I had a nose ring—I loved it," says Rhea, age eighteen, from Massachusetts.

> I liked the attention it got me, but mostly I liked having something everyone didn't have. At first glance, it said: "I don't look like everyone else." For me, it was a small rebellion against society since I'm a girl who is "preppy" and not the type to have one [a piercing]. It meant I didn't have to live by the rules or regulations—it was one of

those things you own and no one can take it away—for teens, there's little in life that's just your own. The thing I think is scary is to do it [piercing] because it's trendy—then when you are left alone, you find it isn't what you wanted.

In recent years, body piercings have replaced tattoos—and even hairstyles—as the latest expression of individuality. Some observers see this trend as a conscious attempt to repudiate Western norms and values. Frustrated with a world that they feel powerless to change, people turn to whatever they do have power over—in this case, their own bodies. Author Mark Edmundson associates body piercing with a rebirth of the Gothic esthetic and its dark, pessimistic view of the world.[17] Other analysts tie it to a New Age celebration of and focus on the self—a sort of rite of passage ritual without religion.

Most analysts view the whole phenomenon as an adolescent identity struggle. They point to its inspiration by the punk revival, MTV, rock stars, and celebrities like supermodel Christy Turlington, who first sported a navel ring at a Paris fashion show. The 1989 book, *Modern Primitives*, is also credited with contributing greatly to the mainstreaming of modern body piercing.[18]

Body piercing, as opposed to earlobe piercing, is the penetration of jewelry into openings made in such body areas as the eyebrows, lips, tongue, navel, nipples, and genitals. Body piercing in ancient cultures was often done to denote royalty or elitism. As a rite of passage, Egyptian pharaohs traditionally pierced their navels, Africans pierced their noses and

"Piercing is the way to express who I am," explains this modern young woman.

tongues, and American Indian males of some tribes endured a ritual suspension from hooks implanted in their chests. Today in the United States, piercing is a relatively new phenomenon.

Body piercing and tattooing have many things in common. Often the same people seek both procedures. In fact, piercing is routinely done right in many tattoo studios. Like tattooing, piercing is done by unlicensed practitioners. Although they refer to themselves as professionals, these practitioners have learned their trade from other piercers, magazine articles, or videos.

As a rule, the art of body piercing is not regulated by any official health standards, nor enforced by any state or federal government agency. The state of Texas is an exception. It has standardized rules of sanitation and rules of disclosure, which obligate clients to be informed of care procedures and possible risks, and to report any adverse reactions from a procedure. In California, Oregon, and Wisconsin, as in Texas, parental permission is required for getting a piercing at a tattoo studio.

To pierce the body, ear-piercing guns, surgical clamps, forceps, hemostats (instruments for compressing blood vessels), or large-gauge needles are most commonly used. Studio piercers are not qualified to administer anesthesia, but pain is often considered a positive by-product of getting a piercing. Suffering pain likens the ritual to a tribal initiation. In a piercing, the skin site is marked, the skin held by forceps, and the opening made with a hollow needle. The jewelry selected is attached to the needle and pulled through the piercing site. There is usually a small to moderate amount of bleeding.

Risks in Body Piercing

There are many potential health hazards associated with body piercing, depending on the site chosen for the hole. Unlike the earlobe, which contains fatty tissue, many body sites chosen are supplied by major blood vessels and nerve centers. Even upper ear piercing is more complicated than earlobe piercing. Because the upper ear region is mostly cartilage, the pain there is greater and the healing time longer than with fatty tissue.

The tongue is a muscular organ filled with blood vessels. Complications from a tongue piercing can include tooth damage from biting on the jewelry, partial paralysis if the jewelry pierces a nerve, and extreme inflammation during the first few days. One fifteen-year-old girl's tongue was so swollen that she had trouble breathing after an amateur piercer inserted a shank too short to allow for normal swelling.[19]

Nipple, navel, and genitalia piercings penetrate different types of tissue and can produce other problems. These sites, usually covered by clothes, can become infected, either from the clothes chafing the site or from moisture buildup. Nipple piercing can damage lactating ducts, and navel piercings have a tendency to pull out unless they are placed deep enough into the abdominal depression.[20]

If an ear-piercing gun is used on parts of the body other than the earlobe, cartilage can be crushed, needing surgical repair; the jewelry can become imbedded; and gangrene, abscessing, and other infections can develop.[21] People who are susceptible to unusual scarring or to skin infections, such as diabetics, should avoid piercing. Infection is possible at any time after the piercing, because the hardware is difficult to keep clean. Scarring is irreversible.

Marc Lappé warns that since both tattooing and body-piercing practices penetrate the skin, there is always increased opportunity for harmful substances to enter the body. ". . . one of the most valuable lessons you can teach someone is that your skin is very open to the world," says Lappé.[22]

Many of the students surveyed experienced frequent soreness, redness, and occasional puslike drainage from their pierced sites, regardless of the skill level of the artists selected and their level of hygiene.

In addition to health risks, there can be other negative reactions. One student with a tongue piercing removed the inserted barbell and allowed the hole to close because he got tired of people asking what was wrong with his speech.[23] Dr. Barbara Staggers, director of adolescent medicine at Children's Hospital in Oakland, California, advises teens to think about the reasons for getting a piercing. Consider how much of the decision is based on peer pressure. "You need to understand that sometimes what your friends say is absolutely right on the money and sometimes they're way off in left field," she says.

> You need to learn to make decisions for yourself. What's really important is weighing the risks versus the benefits. Asking yourself: "Is this a lifelong decision or . . . something I can reverse?" . . . consider what your motivation is for getting a piercing: "Is there another way for me to feel cool, is there another way for me to be with this peer group or maybe, why is this peer group so important to me?"[24]

Body Focus

Cosmetic surgery, tattooing, and body piercing are all ways to modify or embellish the body. People choose these practices for many reasons, but all of them have to do with enhancing one's body image as a means of establishing a personal identity. This focus on one's body is supposed to reinforce one's own sense of attractiveness, help form an association with a peer group or a cultural model, or help a person rebel against cultural standards.

The real question is, if you fix the body, will the body image be fixed, too? As we have seen, some people are physically imperfect compared with an ideal standard and learn to be satisfied with their appearance. Others remain dissatisfied even after twenty cosmetic surgeries. What else can be done to achieve a positive body image?

7

Accepting
Your Body

Having a good body image isn't about
feeling that you always look great. It's
about being satisfied. When you're satisfied (not necessarily ecstatic) with your
body and overall appearance, you are free
to mature into your full potential as a
human being. When you have only negative thoughts about your body, your body
image can interfere with the development
of your other attributes. While your physical self may develop, your inner being of
thoughts, plans, dreams, and talents
doesn't have a chance to grow as it should.
Then it's even tougher to make a successful crossing into adulthood. It's a little like

trying to cross a street without raising your eyes from the ground—it's hard to see the cars coming or when the light changes.

Transition into adulthood can be tough, but it isn't necessarily negative. Adolescence provides the opportunities to turn change to your advantage.

Tune Out the Bad

One way to develop a healthy body image is to tune out bad influences on how you feel about your looks. Author Jill S. Zimmerman offers,

> Unfortunately, we can't wave a magic wand to make our culture more sensitive to our needs. But we can change our own attitudes: we can refuse to take the media so seriously, and we can challenge the images and their devaluing messages.[1]

Film star Alicia Silverstone was heavily criticized by the media in 1996 when she put on a few pounds. "More 'Babe' than babe," screamed a *People* magazine cover headline referring to the movie about a pig named Babe. However, Silverstone refused to let the media's comments about her weight gain change her attitude. In a *Seventeen* magazine interview Silverstone stated, "I didn't become anorexic because somebody said I was heavy. And I didn't become bulimic, and I didn't start dieting. . . this is what I was before, this is what I am now, and this is what I will always be. You either like it or you don't."[2]

Kate Winslet, star of the megahit movie *Titanic*, knows how Silverstone feels. In the March 16, 1998 issue of *People* magazine, she tells her interviewer she no longer worries so much about her impression on others. "The way she looks? 'Like it or lump it!'"[3]

Learn to tune out television programs and commercials that promote unrealistic body types. If you can't tune them out, at least develop a critical eye and ear—recognize the messages that either promote one body type or are demeaning to women or men. Or, better still, laugh at these messages. Think about how boring the world would be with one race, one type of food, one hairstyle, one political party. Variety enriches life. Why, then, do we buy into the concept of one body type? When you become aware of what's really being promoted, it is easy to see how ridiculous it is for TV programs and commercials to pretend to represent real life.

Tune out magazine advertisements and articles that make you unhappy with your body. Don't buy magazines that promote negative stereotypes of women or men. Remember that articles such as "How to Have a Perfect Body" are published to help sell magazines, not to actually expect results. Read magazines that focus on topics other than appearance, or balance your reading materials. One teen in our survey likes to read *Seventeen*, but she also reads *Newsweek*.

Likewise, tune out peers who constantly focus their negative attention on their bodies or yours. Some peer evaluation is normal, even helpful, but if it becomes an obsession, it's time to count yourself out and do something more uplifting. Dating someone who makes negative comments about your weight or shape is also unhealthy for your body image and self-esteem. Rethink your relationships to see if you are surrounding yourself with people who spend too much time focusing on each other's—and your—appearance.

Tune out negative inner messages. One therapist suggests that you should imagine saying to a friend all the hateful things you say to your own body every day. The therapist then asks, "How many friends would you have left?"[4] Experts advise changing self-talk from negative to positive and to stop focusing on the body parts that you don't like. Stop comparing your body with others. Look at your body as unique, not inferior to some other ideal. Focus, instead, on what your body parts can do for you. For instance, you may not like your thighs, but realize what they can do—walk, run, take you up mountain trails. Then, when you're ready, you'll be able to see what, if anything, you can do for them.

Turn On to Life

Turn on to ideals, moral not physical. Adolescence is a time to think about what life is all about and to develop a set of values that gives your life purpose. One of the problems with focusing too much attention on your body is that you fail to develop the spiritual and intellectual parts of yourself.

"A word I use a lot now with patients is 'soulfulness,'" says Carolyn Costin, director of the Eating Disorder Center of Malibu, California, who adds that teenagers need a connection "to what's really good and nourishing for the soul."[5] When people feel that

Peers greatly influence the way teens feel about themselves. "Friends are those who I can laugh and enjoy myself with," says Lindsey, age sixteen.

life has meaning and purpose, they have a foundation from which to look at other aspects of living. Therapist and author Mary Pipher writes: "Many of the great idealists of history, such as Anne Frank and Joan of Arc, were adolescent girls."[6] Rabbi Steve Cohen of Hillel at the University of California at Santa Barbara cites a famous Jewish saying: "In a place where there are no humans, strive to be a human being."[7]

Turn on to helping others. Many teens find that volunteering brings them a great sense of worth and accomplishment. "I like helping others," says Christina, age thirteen. "It helps me feel like I'm making a difference," says Leanne, age seventeen. Rhea, age eighteen, finds it rewarding to go to Kentucky with her church group every year to help build homes for people who have lost theirs to fire or flood. Projects such as Teen Outreach and Maryland's unique statewide community service program for teens (a requirement for high school graduation there) provide a way to contribute to society. Maryland high school senior Brent Rademacher found teaching swimming to disabled children who are training for the Special Olympics so rewarding that he plans to continue the activity on his own.[8]

Turn on to exercise—for fun and fitness, not just to lose weight. Caitlin, age thirteen, says, "Our bodies were meant to be used. Sports are fun, give you higher self-esteem and better health." Exercise can dramatically lift your spirits, as well as your body image. Exercise is probably the easiest way to take control of your body. In addition to the obvious increased health benefits (it positively impacts every part of your body, lowers cholesterol, strengthens the heart and other muscles, and relieves stress), exercise releases endorphins in the brain. These are natural chemicals that make you feel good. Furthermore, exercise can be done according to your own schedule and requirements. If you don't like team sports, you

"*Sports are important to me. Our bodies were meant to be used, and sports are fun, give you higher self-esteem, and help your health,*" *says Caitlin, age thirteen.*

can ride a bike, climb a mountain, or just take a walk. "I started walking every day for about an hour," says a young New Yorker. "Because I was walking I felt so good. I also lost ten pounds, but that didn't matter. My attitude changed because I cared about my health."

Turn on to special activities, talents, clubs, time with family and friends. Those who have a broad range of interests generally cope better with the stresses of life than those who are more limited. Activities also broaden your possibilities for the future—many people begin a hobby that ends up being a vocation. "Singing and dancing are my very most favorite things to do," says Sara, age thirteen, "'cause they help me to be happy."

Try to find your strongest talent, suggests one writer, and use it. She ought to know. Like many other girls, Rebecca Barry wanted to be on the pages of *Seventeen* magazine when she was a teenager. She admits that if she had relied on her face or body to get there, she never would have made it. Instead Barry used her other abilities—in this case, writing—and ended up writing a monthly column for every issue of the magazine.[9]

"Art is what I do to relieve my mind and it gives me goals," comments Leanne, age seventeen, from Wisconsin. Special interest or service clubs provide places to volunteer or to socialize. "Clubs are ways to meet other people," according to Katie, age fifteen, of Nevada. "Make and keep great friends," advises Megan, age thirteen, from Ohio. Lindsey, age fifteen, from California, says that the best friends are those who "have the ability to listen, are easy to get along with, you can laugh and enjoy yourself with, make you feel confident in yourself and understand you."

Work on the things you can change and forget what you can't—and develop the wisdom to know the difference. As television actress Marcella Lowery

People who have lots of interests have a healthier self-concept.

says, "Learn to love yourself for your unique beauty. Rejoice in the fact that there's no one like you."[10] You can't change your genetic body shape or certain parts you might like to, but you can change the way you relate to other people.

Sally, a junior in high school, was shy and lacked confidence about her looks. She tried to avoid eye contact with anyone as she hurried between classes. Then she began to think about something she had heard, about being the first person to say "hello." She began to try to look at the people she passed, smile, and be the first to say "hello." At first, it was hard and sometimes she felt like an idiot, especially when she didn't get a response. But as time went on, it became easier, and Sally was surprised to find other people saying "hello" first. She still felt shy, but she was beginning to get a new feeling about herself.

Ed Wimberly, a family therapist, says,

> Teens buy into a bill of goods that many of us accept: If you want to act a certain way, you need to feel it first. This is wrong. If you want to feel a certain way, start acting that way first, the feelings will follow. Some kids might think this is hypocritical, but it's not. It's the motivation that's important.[11]

A successful businessman puts it this way: "Fake it 'til you make it."

Talk to Others

Don't be afraid to talk to friends, family, teachers, and coaches about body image issues. Sometimes friends are struggling with exactly the same problems you are. Try to encourage your friends to be sensitive about other people's appearances.

Talk to friends of the opposite sex. Maybe they haven't really thought about how much their views of others' body shapes and sizes are influenced by our culture. When they make negative comments about weight or stature, ask them to consider the effects their casual remarks may have.

Talk to parents and other family members about how you feel—especially if you are struggling with a negative body image. Sometimes parents fail to pick up on clues that are obvious to you. Maybe they have no idea how much their remarks may be hurting you. Let them know. If necessary, have them help you seek outside counseling.

Talk to coaches or teachers who might be putting pressure on you or others to conform to a certain weight or size. The subject of body image is often covered in classes in family health. If your school doesn't include this issue in its curriculum, you might suggest it as a topic. Joanna Deeter, the Notre Dame cross-country runner who struggled with anorexia nervosa, organized an eating-disorder group at her school to help educate others on campus.[12]

Don't ignore your bad feelings—sometimes just getting them out in the open helps. Talk to a school counselor if you can't talk to your friends or family, or if you find that you can't seem to resolve your negative feelings about yourself. Or call the hotlines or organizations listed in the back of this book. There is always someone, somewhere, who can help you.

Body image is a complicated matter. It is much

Accomplishing goals with our bodies is more important than focusing on how they look.

more than what you see in the mirror. It involves a whole spectrum of feelings about yourself. There's never been anything wrong with trying to look your best, with being interested in clothes and style, and with putting things together to change the way you look to give yourself a body-image boost. All those outward adjustments can help improve the way you feel about yourself. However, it's important to remember that the most essential part of a person is who you are on the inside. If you can be "at home in your body," you will be free to discover just who lives inside.

Glossary

adolescence—A stage of development prior to maturity.

anemia—A condition in which the blood is deficient in red blood cells, hemoglobin, or in total volume.

cessation—An end.

cleft palate—A long, deep crack in the roof of the mouth which is first evident at birth.

ecstatic—Very happy.

electrolyte—One of the dissolved substances found in water that regulates many processes in cells.

embellish—To enhance.

esthetic—A particular theory or conception of beauty or art.

euphoria—A feeling of well-being.

heredity—The transmission of qualities from ancestor to descendant through genes.

hype—Publicity which makes something appear more important than it actually is.

metabolism—The chemical changes in cells by which energy is provided for vital processes and activities and new material is absorbed into the body's systems.

norm—A standard.

phobia—An intense fear.

repudiate—To refuse to accept.

self-inspection—To evaluate oneself.

stringent—Strict.

subconscious—Existing in the mind, but not immediately available to the conscious, or thinking, process.

synthetic—Not occurring naturally; man-made.

Resources

Body Piercing and Tattooing

Association of Professional Piercers
519 Castro Street, Box 120
San Francisco, CA 94114
e-mail: app@sfo.com

Alliance of Professional Tattooists—APT
P.O. Box 1735
Glen Burnie, MD 21060
(410) 768-1963

Body piercing information and after-care instruction:
<http://www.gauntlet.com> (August 18, 1998).

Tattoo Informational Video:
A Tattoo . . . YOU? Teens Talking to Teens, video
Texas Tech University Health Sciences Center
School of Nursing
Attn: Carolyn Miller
3601 Fourth Street, Room 2B164
Lubbock, Texas.

Tattoo removal:
<www.bme.freeq.com/tattoo/tr/index.html> (August 18, 1998). (For gang-related tattoo removal, contact TagAway, a program that provides free tattoo removal in exchange for community service <www.tagaway.com/projects.html> (August 18, 1998).

Cosmetic Surgery

Plastic surgery information:
America Online Media Center
<http://www.plasticsurgery.org> (August 18, 1998).

Dieting and Eating Disorders

American Anorexia/Bulimia Association (AA/BA)
165 W. 46th Street, Suite 1108
New York, NY 10036
(212) 575-6200

Anorexia Nervosa and Related Eating Disorders (ANRED)
P.O. Box 5102
Eugene, OR 97405
(541) 344-1144
<http://www.anred.com> (August 18, 1998).

Eating Disorders Awareness and Prevention (ADAP)
603 Stewart Street, Suite 803
Seattle, WA 98101
(206) 382-3587

Hugs International: Teens and Diet: No Weigh
<http://www.hugs.com> (August 18, 1998).

National Association of Anorexia Nervosa and Associated Disorders (ANAD)
P.O. Box 7
Highland Park, IL 60035
(708) 831-3438

National Eating Disorders Organization (NEDO)
6655 South Yale Avenue
Tulsa, OK 74136
(918) 481-4044

Overeaters Anonymous
6075 Zenith Court
Rio Rancho, NM 87124
(505) 891-2664
Fax: (505) 891-4320
e-mail: overeatr@technet.nm.org.

For Boys

Information on health issues
<http://www.menshealth.com> (August 18, 1998).

For Girls

Girls Incorporated
National Resource Center
441 West Michigan Street
Indianapolis, IN 40101
(317) 634-7546

Size Esteem:

**Association for the Health Enrichment
for Large People (AHELP)**
P.O. Box 11743
Blacksburg, VA 24072-1743
(540) 951-3527

**Idrea—the Larger Woman's Workout,
47-minute collage video**
(800) 433-6769

Largesse: The Network for Size Esteem
(203) 787-1624

**National Association to Advance Fat Acceptance
(NAAFA)**
(800) 442-1214

Volunteer Programs

Teen Outreach Program
Cornerstone Consulting Group
1 Greenway Plaza, Suite 550
Houston, TX 77046
(713) 627-2322

Chapter Notes

Chapter 1. Body Image—What, Exactly, Is It?

1. Seymour Fisher, *The Development and Structure of the Body Image* (Hillsdale, N.J.: Lawrence Erlbaum Associates, Inc., 1986), p. 316.

2. David M. Garner, Ann Kearney-Cooke, "Body Image 1996," *Psychology Today*, March–April 1996, p. 56.

3. Susan Spaeth Cherry, "Rebels Without Taste," *The Los Angeles Times*, April 6, 1997, p. E3.

4. Erik H. Erikson, *Identity and the Life Cycle* (New York: W. W. Norton & Company, 1980), pp. 127–128.

5. Personal interview with Jon Ireland, youth pastor, Montecito Covenant Church, Montecito, Calif., November 28, 1996.

6. Emily Hancock, as quoted in Jane E. Brody, "Girls and Puberty: the Crisis Years," *The New York Times*, November 4, 1997, p. F9.

7. Carole Wade and Carol Tavris, *Psychology* (New York: HarperCollins College Publishers, 1993), p. 512.

8. Jill Neimark, "The Beefcaking of America," *Psychology Today*, November–December 1994, p. 35.

9. Questionnaire, Santa Barbara Junior High School, Calif., May 5, 1997.

10. Lauren Tarshis, "Your Body, Your Self," *Choices*, January 1995, p. 12.

Chapter 2. Influences on Image: Societal, Peer, and Media Pressures

1. Joanne Ikeda and Priscilla Naworski, *Am I Fat? Helping Children Accept Differences in Body Size* (Santa Cruz, Calif.: ETR Associates, 1992), pp. 7–9.

2. Lauren Tarshis, "Your Body, Your Self," *Choices*, January 1995, p. 9.

3. Stephanie Dolgoff, "You Don't Have to Be Thin to Be Hot," *YM Special*, 1997, p. 40.

4. Personal interview with Tim Connelly, University of Notre Dame, South Bend, Ind., December 18, 1997.

5. Judith Rodin, *Body Traps: Breaking the Binds That Keep You From Feeling Good About Your Body* (New York: William Morrow and Company, 1992), p. 109.

6. Personal interview with Jon Ireland, youth pastor, Montecito Covenant Church, Montecito, Calif., November 28, 1996.

7. Walt Mueller, *Understanding Today's Youth Culture* (Wheaton, Ill.: Tyndale House Publishers, 1994), p. 146.

8. Nancy Signorelli, "Reflections of Girls in the Media: A Content Analysis Across Six Media," *Report*, The Kaiser Family Foundation and Children Now, April 1997.

9. Michael P. Levine and Linda Smolak, "Media as a Context for the Development of Disordered Eating," *The Developmental Psychopathology of Eating Disorders: Implications for Research, Prevention, and Treatment*, ed. Linda Smolak, Michael P. Levine, and Ruth Striegel-Moore (Mahwah, N.J.: Lawrence Erlbaum Associates, 1996), p. 243.

10. Leslie Morgan, "Why Are Girls Obsessed with Their Weight?," *Seventeen*, November 1989, p. 145.

11. Ellen Goodman, "Thin Models Crossing the Line," *Santa Barbara News-Press*, June 11, 1996, p. A9.

12. Michael Levine, "Beauty, Myth and the Beast: What Men Can Do and Be to Help Prevent Eating Disorders," *Eating Disorders*, Summer 1994, p. 106.

13. Levine and Smolak, p. 243.

14. Personal interview with Michael Levine, professor of psychology, Kenyon College, Ohio, and president, Eating Disorders Awareness and Prevention, February 2, 1997.

15. Linda Ellerbee, "The Body Trap," "Nick News Special Edition," *Nickelodeon*, May 29, 1996.

16. Candace A. Wedlan, "Don't Hate Her Because She's Slender," *The Los Angeles Times*, October 30, 1996, p. F1.

Chapter 3. A Short History of the Human Form

1. Nancy Signorelli, "Reflections of Girls in the Media: A Content Analysis Across Six Media," The Kaiser Family Foundation and Children Now, April 1997.

2. Lois W. Banner, *American Beauty* (New York: Alfred A. Knopf, 1983), p. 228.

3. Ibid., pp. 286–287.

4. Zibby Schwarzman, "My Weight, Myself," *Seventeen*, August 1993, p. 102.

Chapter 4. Eating Disorders: Serious Problems for Teenagers

1. Leslie Morgan, "Why Are Girls So Obsessed with Their Weight?" *Seventeen*, November 1989, p. 119.

2. Christine Gombar, "I Was a Teenage Waif," *Choices*, January 1994, p. 4.

3. Eva Pomice, "I'm So Fat! When Kids Hate Their Bodies," *Redbook*, April 1995, p. 185.

4. David M. Garner, "Results of 1996 Body Image Survey," *Psychology Today*, January/February 1997, p. 38.

5. Margo Maine, "The Pressure on Children," reprinted by EDAP, Seattle, Wash., from *Eating Disorders in Focus*, Newington Children's Hospital, Newington, Conn.

6. Emily Hancock, as quoted in Jane E. Brody, "Girls and Puberty: the Crisis Years," *The New York Times*, November 4, 1997, p. F9.

7. Naomi Wolf, *The Beauty Myth: How Images of Beauty Are Used Against Women* (New York: Anchor Books, Doubleday, 1992) p. 192.

8. Personal interview with Monika Wooley, president of Better Way Health Control, Phoenix, Ariz., June 14, 1997.

9. Brett Valette, *A Parent's Guide to Eating Disorders: Prevention and Treatment of Anorexia Nervosa and Bulimia* (New York: Walker Publishing Company, 1988), pp. 15–16.

10. Judith Rodin, *Body Traps: Breaking the Binds That Keep You From Feeling Good About Your Body* (New York: William Morrow and Company, 1992), p. 177.

11. Paula Levine, "Background Material for Presentations: The Meaning of the 3 D's" printout from EDAP, Seattle, Wash.

12. Ibid.

13. Jane E. Brody, "Old Diet Fad Is Back but It Still Doesn't Work," *Santa Barbara News-Press*, December 31, 1996, p. D-1.

14. Barbara Thomas, "Then and Now," *The Los Angeles Times*, January 5, 1998, p. S-1.

15. "Body Image," IMS Productions, *NavPress Youth Specialties*, edition 1, 1991.

16. Seymour Fisher, *The Development and Structure of the Body Image* (Hillsdale, N.J.: Lawrence Erlbaum Associates, 1986), p. 182.

17. Personal interview with Carolyn Costin, director, Eating Disorder Center of California, Malibu, October 9, 1997.

18. Donald L. Greydanus, ed., *Caring for Your Adolescent: Ages 12 to 21* (New York: Bantam Books, 1991), p. 242.

19. American Academy of Pediatrics, *Eating Disorders: What You Should Know About Anorexia and Bulimia—Guidelines for Teens* (Elk Grove, Ill.: 1996).

20. Ibid.

21. Jane R. Hirschmann, CSW, and Lela Zaphiropoulos, CSW, *Preventing Childhood Eating Problems* (Carlsbad, Calif.: Gürze Books, 1993), pp. 148–150.

22. Costin interview.

23. Kathy McCoy and Charles Wibbelsman, *The New Teenage Body Book* (New York: The Body Press/Perigee, Putnam Publishing Group, 1992), p. 163.

24. Costin interview.

25. McCoy and Wibbelsman, p. 162.

Chapter 5. Fears, Steroids, and Muscle Mania

1. David M. Garner, "The 1997 Body Image Survey Results," *Psychology Today*, February 1997, p. 38.

2. Kathy McCoy and Charles Wibbelsman, *The New Teenage Body Book* (New York: The Body Press/Perigee, Putnam Publishing Group, 1992), p. 53.

3. Nancy Wride, "Eau de P.E.," *The Los Angeles Times*, October, 2, 1996, p. E8.

4. Ibid., p. E8.

5. McCoy and Wibbelsman, p. 53.

6. Jennifer Perrillo, "Muscle Madness," *Choices*, January 1995, p. 13.

7. Jill Neimark, "The Beefcaking of America," *Psychology Today*, November/December 1994, p. 70.

8. Amy B. Middleman, Annie H. Faulkner, Elizabeth R. Woods, S. Jean Emans, and Robert H. DuRant, "High-Risk Behaviors Among High School Students in

Massachusetts Who Use Anabolic Steroids," *Pediatrics*, 1995, p. 269.

9. Personal interview with Steven Anderson, chair, Committee on Sports Medicine and Fitness, American Academy of Pediatrics, March 25, 1997.

10. Lawrence G. Proulx, "Want a Better Body? Then Work at It," *The Los Angeles Times*, May 30, 1997, p. E4.

11. Steven J. Anderson, "Adolescents and Anabolic Steroids: A Subject Review," *Pediatrics*, June 1997, p. 905.

12. Ibid.

13. Anderson interview.

14. Ibid.

15. Ibid.

Chapter 6. Cosmetic Surgery, Tattoos, and Body Piercing

1 Charles Siebert, "The Cuts That Go Deeper," *The New York Times Magazine*, July 7, 1996, p. 25.

2. Judith Rodin, *Body Traps: Breaking the Binds That Keep You From Feeling Good About Your Body* (New York: William Morrow and Company, 1992), p. 26.

3. Marc Lappé, *The Body's Edge: Our Cultural Obsession With Skin* (New York: Henry Holt and Company, 1996), pp. 25–26.

4. Personal interview with Dr. John Persing, professor and chief of plastic surgery, Yale University Medical School, New Haven, Conn., April 21, 1997.

5. Myrna L. Armstrong, and Cathy McConnell, "Tattooing in Adolescents: More Common Than You Think—The Phenomenon and Risks," *Journal of School Nursing*, February 1994, p. 27.

6. Myrna L. Armstrong and Kathleen Pace Murphy, "Tattooing: Another Adolescent Risk-Behavior Warranting

Health Education," *Applied Nursing Research*, November 10, 1997, p. 182.

7. Personal interview with Myrna L. Armstrong, professor, School of Nursing, Texas Tech University Health Sciences Center, Lubbock, June 6, 1997.

8. Myrna L. Armstrong, research notes; used by permission.

9. Armstrong and McConnell, p. 30.

10. Armstrong and Murphy, pp. 184–188.

11. Ibid., p. 182.

12. Personal interview with Dr. Steven Popkow, Santa Monica, Calif., February 8, 1997.

13. Laura Ronge, "Pediatricians' Piercing Insight Can Help Teens Get the Point," *American Academy of Pediatrics News*, January 1997, p. 10.

14. Armstrong and McConnell, p. 27, and Armstrong and Murphy, pp. 186–187.

15. Popkow interview.

16. Ronge, p. 11.

17. Michiko Kakutani, "Why Do Americans Gorge on Gothic?" *The New York Times*, November 14, 1997, p. E4.

18. Myrna Armstrong, Elaine Ekmark, and Barbara Brooks, "Body Piercing: Promoting Informed Decision Making," *Journal of School Nursing*, April 1995, p. 21.

19. Ronge, p. 10.

20. Armstrong, Ekmark, and Brooks, p. 21.

21. "What's Wrong with the Ear-Piercing Gun?—Ask a Piercing Pro," *Gauntlet PWAP*, America Online, <http:/www.gauntlet.com>, pp. 1–2.

22. Shari Roan, "Save Your Skin," *The Los Angeles Times*, July 24, 1996, p. E6.

23. Armstrong, Ekmark, and Brooks, p. 23.

24. Personal interview with Dr. Barbara Staggers, medical director, Adolescent Medicine, Children's Hospital, Oakland, Calif., February 13, 1997.

Chapter 7. Accepting Your Body

1. Jill S. Zimmerman, "An Image to Heal," *The Humanist*, 57, January/February 1997, p. 25.

2. April P. Bernard, "Really, Really Alicia," *Seventeen*, August 1997, p. 207.

3. Jeffrey Wells, Joanna Blonska, and Jason Lynch, "The Love Boat," *People*, March 16, 1998, p. 54.

4. Laura Fraser, "Learning to Love the Mirror," *Health*, March/April 1995, p. 34.

5. Personal interview with Carolyn Costin, director, Eating Disorder Center of California, Malibu, October 9, 1997.

6. Mary Pipher, *Reviving Ophelia: Saving the Selves of Adolescent Girls* (New York: Ballantine Books, 1994), p. 71.

7. Personal interview with Rabbi Steve Cohen, Hillel, University of California at Santa Barbara, June 19, 1997.

8. Lynn Smith, "Pride in Service," *The Los Angeles Times*, June 16, 1997, p. E1.

9. Rebecca Barry, "Body Obsessed," *Seventeen*, July 1995, p. 115.

10. Marcella Lowery and LaShirl Smith of "Absolute...PR!" Sherman Oaks, Calif., October 28, 1997.

11. Personal interview with Ed Wimberly, family therapist, Santa Barbara, Calif., May 22, 1997.

12. Dick Patrick, "Notre Dame Runner Battles Eating Disorder," *USA Today*, October 8, 1997, p. 9C.

Further Reading

Body Image

Bowen-Woodward, Kathryn. *Coping With a Negative Body Image.* New York: Rosen Publishing Group, 1989.

Emme, Daniel Paisner (contributor). *True Beauty: Positive Attitudes and Practical Tips from the World's Leading Plus-Size Model.* New York: Putnam Publishing Group, 1997.

Freedman, Rita. *Body Love: Learning to Like Our Looks and Ourselves.* New York: HarperCollins, 1988.

Hirschman, Jane and Carol Munter. *When Women Stop Hating Their Bodies: Freeing Yourself From Food and Weight Obsession.* Chatwood, N.S.W.: Mandarin, 1995.

Hutchinson, Marcia Germaine. *Transforming Body Image.* Trumansburg, New York: Crossing Press, 1985.

Newman, Leslea. *SomeBody to Love: A Guide to Loving the Body You Have.* Chicago: Third Sided Press, 1991.

Zerbe, Kathryn. *The Body Betrayed.* Carlsbad, Calif.: Gurze Books, 1993.

Dieting and Eating Disorders

Berry, Joy. *Good Answers to Tough Questions About Weight Problems and Eating Disorders.* Chicago: Children's Press, 1990.

Costin, Carolyn. *Your Dieting Daughter: Is She Dying for Attention?* New York: Brunner/Mazel, 1996.

Daum, Michelle, with Amy Lemley. *The Can-Do Eating Plan for Overweight Kids and Teens*. New York: Avon Books, 1997.

Kane, June K. *Coping with Diet Fads*. New York: Rosen Publishing Group, 1990.

Kubersky, Rachel. *Everything You Need to Know About Eating Disorders: Anorexia and Bulimia*. New York, Rosen Publishing Group, 1996.

Landau, Elaine. *Weight, A Teenage Concern*. New York: Lodestar Books, 1991.

Silverstein, Alvin. *So You Think You're Fat?* New York: HarperCollins Children's Books, 1991.

Cultural Influences

Media and Values, quarterly publication, Center for Media and Values, 1962 South Shenendoah Street, Los Angeles, CA 90034.

Still Killing Us Softly, a video on sexist advertising, Cambridge Documentary Films, P.O. Box 385, Cambridge, MA 02139, (617) 354-3677.

Media Guide for Black Girls, National Black Child Development Institute, 1023 15th Street N.W., Suite 600, Washington, DC 20005, (202) 387-1281.

Index